ACTS

A SELF-STUDY GUIDE

Irving L. Jensen

MOODY PRESS

CHICAGO

Contents

Introduction

The study of a book of the Bible involves two approaches, in this order: survey of the whole and analysis of the parts. In survey, the main movements of the composition of the book are searched for in the large units of chapters and groups of chapters. In analysis, the study concentrates on the parts of a chapter, which are paragraphs, sentences, phrases, and words.

The lessons of this study guide, after the first lesson on background and survey, proceed through the book of Acts chapter by chapter or, more accurately, segment by segment.[1] The main method of study fostered in each particular lesson is paragraph by paragraph, for it is believed that this is the most efficient and fruitful approach in Bible analysis. The main parts of each lesson are:

1. *Paragraph divisions*
The verse references supplied here tell where each paragraph begins. Mark these divisions clearly in your Bible, so that as you read you will be paragraph conscious.

2. *Observations and questions*
The study questions given in this section are worded so as to encourage you to do independent study and to look for more than just the obvious truths. Also you are constantly reminded to look for the *main* truths of each segment (or chapter) and paragraph. The reason for this emphasis is that it is very easy to lose sight of the "forest" when one begins to examine each of the many "trees." This is a serious pitfall in the study of any book. Typical questions for this section are:

What is the principal subject of this (segment, paragraph)?
Who are the principal persons in this (segment, paragraph)?
What does the (segment, paragraph) teach concerning Christ?

1. A unit of study longer or shorter than a chapter is here called a segment.

What are key verses in this segment?

What is the leading lesson of this segment?

3. *Applications*

In order that you may be constantly reminded that the application of the Bible to life is the ultimate purpose of Bible study, a space is devoted in each lesson for you to record these applications:

an example to follow

a sin to avoid

a command to obey

a promise to claim

a prayer to echo

Truth should not only be clearly seen but also applied to the heart and life. It is a dangerous thing to ask God to show an example that one should follow and then fail to follow it; or a promise to claim and then fail to claim it.

Prayerful study is of supreme importance. If one seeks the Holy Spirit's guidance, He will reveal the truths that He wants the reader to learn.

4. *A topical study*

At the end of each lesson appears a brief study of a major doctrine of the Bible. The topic chosen is suggested by a word or phrase in the passage being studied in that lesson. The outline and description given is not intended to be exhaustive but rather to encourage further study in the subject. Be sure to read all Bible references cited in this section.

5. *A final thought*

The thought suggested here concerns a truth of the passage. Let it also serve as a reminder to review the things you have studied in the lesson.

Suggestions to leaders of classes

1. The object of this Bible study manual is to encourage the reader to study the Bible for himself, not only to read what someone else has studied. Therefore insist that the members of your class work out answers to the questions on the chapter assigned, at home, before coming to the class.

2. The leader should lead, not lecture to, the class. The charm of this method of study is the exchange of thought by the class members. Therefore the leader should let the members give the results of their study on each point first, before giving his own thoughts.

Also the members should not be led to think that their answers must always agree with the teacher's in order to be correct. For example, each of two different verses may qualify as a key verse of a chapter. Class members should be urged to share their findings, regardless of whether or not their answers agree with everyone else's.

3. The leader should adapt the study to the ability of the class. If the class is composed of people unaccustomed to formal study, simplify the work, at least to begin with, by requiring answers to only one or two of the easier questions, such as selecting the best verse or finding an example to be followed. It is amazing what other precious truths are discovered while looking for a "favorite" verse. Then gradually the members could be led on to study the other points. The important thing is to get everyone to study and think for himself, not merely to absorb what someone else has thought out.

4. The use of charts, maps, and chalkboard is very helpful. Charts enable the Bible student to see the large movements (survey) while he is studying the smaller parts (analysis). Charts are also helpful for review purposes. Never start a new lesson without reviewing the previous one.

5. Encourage the memorizing of Scripture. Have the class commit to memory the verse in each chapter chosen as the best by the majority of the class. Review these verses frequently.

Only a limited treatment of the story of Acts can be made by this study guide due to space limitations. It is hoped that by using this guide the reader will be inspired to make an even fuller study of this key book of the New Testament. Those who are interested in getting help to make such a comprehensive analysis are referred to the author's book *Acts: An Inductive Study*.[2]

> The **Acts** is a Book of Origins. Here are the beginnings of the Christian Church, of apostolic miracles, of apostolic sermons, of Christian persecution, of Christian martyrs, of Gentile converts, of disciplinary judgment in the Church, of Church Synods, of Foreign Missions, of Christian Baptism and Christian Assemblies, and of the denomination "Christian." **Acts** is a dawn, a glorious sunrise, a bursting forth in a dark world of eternal light; it is a Book precious beyond all price.[3]

2. Irving L. Jensen, *Acts: An Inductive Study* (Chicago: Moody, 1968).
3. W. Graham Scroggie, *Know Your Bible* (London: Pickering & Inglis, n.d.), 2:76-77.

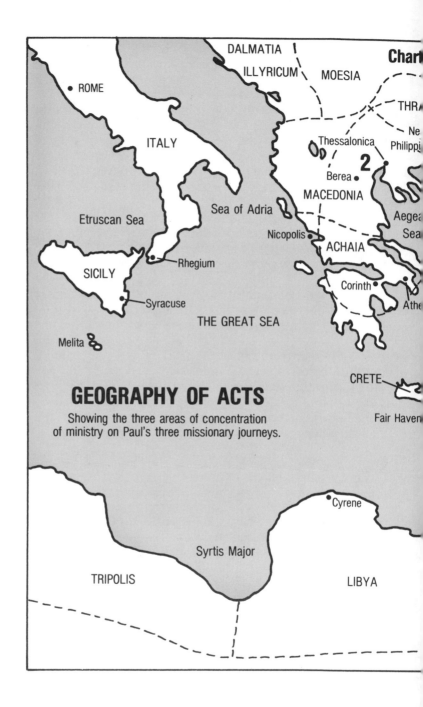

GEOGRAPHY OF ACTS

Showing the three areas of concentration
of ministry on Paul's three missionary journeys.

Pontus Euxinus

THRACE

PONTUS

BITHYNIA

GALATIA

CAPPADOCIA

Troas

MYSIA

3

PHRYGIA

LYDIA

1

Ephesus

Antioch

Iconium

Colosse

Lystra

CILICIA

PAMPHYLIA

Derbe

Tarsus

LYCIA

Perga

ANTIOCH

Rhodes

CYPRUS

Salamis

Paphos

Damascus

SYRIA

THE GREAT SEA

Sidon

PALESTINE

Caesarea

Joppa

JERUSALEM

ALEXANDRIA

ARABIA

EGYPT

Lesson 1
Background of Acts

Before analyzing the text of any book of the Bible, it is well to learn the historical background. Also, it is best to take a "sky-scraper" view of its general contents. Accordingly, this first lesson is divided into two parts: background and survey.

I. BACKGROUND

At the very outset of our study these are some of the questions that come to mind: Who wrote the book? When did he write it? What was his main object? What is the historical setting? How does the book serve a particular function in the entire Bible? The answers to these and other questions are given briefly below.

A. Name

The short name usually assigned the book is "Acts." The full name "Acts of the Apostles" is traceable back to the second century. When the book was originally written, its author, Luke, probably combined it with his earlier writing, the gospel of Luke. Then when his gospel was joined to the other three gospels, Acts stood alone. Here are some observations.

1. The key word in the longer title is *Acts*. These are not the dreams, theories, or speculations of the apostles, but their acts, their deeds, things they actually accomplished. Anyone who denies the divine power manifested in the early church must deny the factuality of the acts of this book.

2. The phrase "of the apostles" probably refers to the main apostles of the years of the book's record. Of these apostles, Peter and Paul were the key leaders.

3. It is recognized that the book records the acts of the Holy Spirit as He worked through the apostles. In that sense the book

could be called The Acts of the Holy Spirit. The Holy Spirit's name appears about seventy times in the book.

B. Author

Luke is the author (cf. Acts 1:1 with Luke 1:1-4). He was a Gentile about the same age as Paul and was his constant companion for about the last twenty years of Paul's life. Paul probably led Luke to the Lord. Luke was a gifted scholar and physician, and from his Christian life shined forth such admirable traits as kindness, loyalty, faith, and exuberance. New Testament references to him (outside of Acts) are Colossians 4:14; Philemon 24; 2 Timothy 4:11. Read these.

C. Date Written

Luke apparently finished writing Acts around A.D. 61 while Paul was still imprisoned in Rome (Acts 28). The Holy Spirit's design was not to include any more of Paul's life or of the church's experience in this book, so He inspired Luke to write at this time.

D. Period Covered

The time span of Acts is about thirty-one years. The narrative begins with Jesus' ascension (A.D. 30) and closes with Paul in prison (A.D. 61). It would be interesting to compare the church's succeeding generations with the one of Acts, as to the advance made in the propagation of the gospel. Some of the later epistles and Revelation 2-3 furnish descriptions for such a comparison.

E. Geographical Centers

The mission assigned to the early church, spelled out in Acts 1:8, was universal. The performance of that mission in the years of Acts retained the universal quality, for the home base of the missionaries kept moving. The advance was generally from east to west: Jerusalem to Antioch (Syria) to Ephesus to Rome. Of the four cities, Acts records the most details in connection with Jerusalem and Antioch.

II. SURVEY

"Image the whole, then execute the parts." This is the correct order in Bible study. We should first get an overview of the book in its large scope, and then study the smaller parts in detail. For the purposes of this short study guide, the following descriptions bring out the highlights of a survey of Acts.

A. The Principal Subject of Acts

Acts is basically a history of the beginnings of Christianity. How significant were those beginnings! The active role of the three Persons of the Godhead[1] at this great period of world history, is indicated in Chart B.

THE ROLE OF THE THREE PERSONS OF THE GODHEAD Chart B

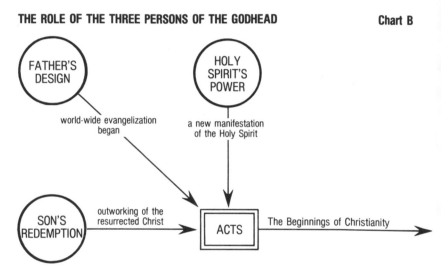

The principal subject of Acts may be identified in other ways. Some of the various titles that could be assigned the book are:

The witness of the gospel

The living Lord in action (In Acts Christ *continues* to do what He *began* to do in the gospels. Cf. Acts 1:1)

The advent and activity of the Holy Spirit

The early church in action

Keep the above mentioned principal subjects in mind as you proceed from chapter to chapter in Acts.

---

1. When a generalization is made concerning the prominent functions of the three Persons of the Godhead during the years of Bible history, it may be said that the Father is most prominent in the Old Testament, the Son in the gospels, and the Holy Spirit in Acts.

B. Place in the Bible

Acts is the sequel to the gospels that precede it and the background to the epistles that follow it. It is the historical record that attests the success of Jesus' earthly ministry by showing how the risen Lord works in the present age in the hearts of men. The explanations and interpretations of the tremendous events of Acts are given in the epistles. Thus it is obvious how important a place Acts fills in the New Testament.

C. A Key Verse

The verse most frequently recognized as the key verse of Acts is 1:8: "But you shall be filled with power when the Holy Spirit comes on you, and you will be witnesses for me in Jerusalem, in all of Judea and Samaria, and to the ends of the earth" (*Good News for Modern Man*).

The words in the middle of this verse "You will be witnesses for me" are both a command and a prophecy. It will be seen in connection with survey Chart C how the church extended its witness in the geographical directions of 1:8.

D. A Key Word

A key word of Acts is "witness," appearing in its various forms about twenty times.

E. Structure

Survey readings of Acts reveal, among other things, the large movements of the book and the major emphases. When all this data is in and worked over, the structure of the book begins to take shape. One way to show this organization is by means of a survey chart. Before you study survey Chart C you should make at least one cursory reading of Acts, observing the highlights and recording a chapter title for each segment shown. Try to choose your chapter titles from the text itself (see examples for chaps. 1 and 2). This will help you develop an awareness of key words and phrases, which are vital tools in Bible study. (Note: Although most of the chapters of Acts are study units beginning with the first verse of those chapters, some segments begin at verses other than the first verse, depending on the narrative. Follow the divisions shown on Chart C). You may choose to make your own survey chart before referring to Chart C.

ACTS THE BEGINNINGS OF CHRISTIANITY

Chart C

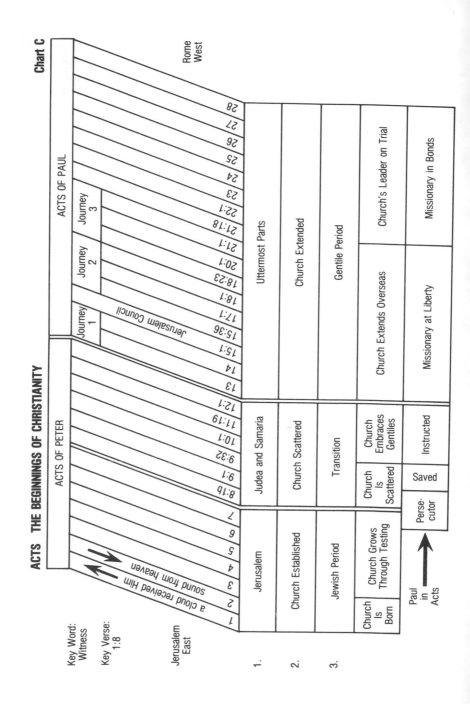

ACTS OF PETER					**ACTS OF PAUL**	
					Journey 1 · Journey 2 · Journey 3	
Jerusalem East				Jerusalem Council		Rome West

Key Word: Witness
Key Verse: 1:8

a cloud received Him
sound from heaven

Chapters: 1 2 3 4 5 6 7 | 8:1b 9:1 9:32 10:1 11:19 12:1 | 13 14 15:1 15:36 17:1 18:1 18:23 20:1 21:1 21:18 22:1 23 24 25 26 27 28

1. Jerusalem | Judea and Samaria | Uttermost Parts

2. Church Established | Church Scattered | Church Extended

3. Jewish Period | Transition | Gentile Period

Church Grows Through Testing | Church Is Scattered | Church Extends Overseas | Church's Leader on Trial

Church Is Born | Church Embraces Gentiles

Perse-cutor | Saved | Instructed | Missionary at Liberty | Missionary in Bonds

Paul in Acts

- **Observations on Chart C**

1. The twenty-eight chapters of Acts fall into three main divisions, with dividing points at 8:1*b* and 13:1. Note the three outlines (1, 2, and 3 on the left side of the chart), which demonstrate this threefold organization. The geographical outline is a natural unfolding of 1:8. The outline on the church shows a progression of the church in the Acts narrative. Read 8:1*b* and 13:1-4 to see how the new divisions begin at those points.

2. Acts can also be divided into two main parts from the standpoint of main characters (see top of Chart C). In chapters 1-12, Peter plays the leading role, whereas in chapters 13-28 everything centers on Paul's activities.

3. Note the divisions related to Jew and Gentile. In the early chapters of Acts, the Jews compose most of the audience of the gospel. In chapters 10-12 the church sees its responsibility to extend the invitation of the gospel to Gentiles as well. From chapter 13 on, the field is the world. The prominent note of Peter's message, delivered to Jews, was "repent" (see 2:36-38). Paul, whose ministry enlarged to include Gentiles (cf. 18:6), emphasized more the positive aspect of conversion, "believe" (see 16:30-31).

4. Paul as a missionary served well when at liberty (13:1–21:17) and remained loyal when in bonds (21:18–28:31). In both situations God's word multiplied, and souls were saved.

As you conclude your study of this first lesson, ponder over the key verse 1:8: "You will be witnesses for me." In that one word "witness' is condensed the whole wisdom of God as to the world-wide work that He would have His people accomplish in this age. We are to be witnesses unto Him; we are to bring the gospel ("glad tidings") to every creature.

Think of the need for witnessing. Someone has said, "Christ alone can save the world, but Christ cannot save the world alone." That is, Christ cannot do this unless He abandons His plan, for His plan is that every believer should be a witness.

Ask yourself the following questions: Am I a living witness for Christ? If not, why not? If I have no witness for Christ, what am I witnessing to? "Of the abundance of the heart . . . [the] mouth speaketh" (Luke 6:45). "He that believeth on me, as the scripture hath said, out of his belly shall flow rivers of living water" (John 7:38). If I have no witness, have I any experience? If there be no stream, is there any spring? If no ray, is there any light?

These are serious and searching questions, which every believer should ponder. "He who has no passion to convert, needs conversion. "The Son of Man came to seek and to save the lost" (Luke 19:10, *Good News for Modern Man*).

15

Lesson 2

Acts 1:1-26

Witnesses for Jesus

The setting of Acts chapter 1 is vividly set forth in the book's open-ing paragraph of verses 1-5. Jesus had accomplished many things in His earthly ministry, which included His atoning death and postresurrection appearances. Now, at the end of forty days of such appearances, He stood before His closest disciples and gave them His parting orders. This was the hour for Him to return bodily to heaven while the disciples were to prepare to move out to the far corners of the earth with the message of the risen Lord.

• **Paragraph Divisions** Read the chapter paragraph by paragraph. New paragraphs begin at verses 1, 6, 12, 15, 23. If this segment is analyzed in two units, those units would be verses 1-14 and 15-26.

• **Observations and Questions**
1. Who are the speakers in the second paragraph (vv. 6-11)?

_____

_____

2. Compare the question about the kingdom (v. 6) with the refer-ence of 3b.

_____

_____

3. Make a study of promise (v. 4), power (v. 8) and prayer (v. 14).

_____

_____

_____

_____

16

4. How does the phrase "witness with us" (v. 22) relate the narrative of 1:15-26 to the previous paragraphs?

_____

_____

5. Who are the principal persons of verses 1-14?

_____

_____

Of verses 15-26?

_____

6. What is the main point of chapter 1?

_____

7. What is taught about Christ in this chapter?

_____

_____

_____

About the Holy Spirit?

_____

_____

Is there any reference to the Father?

_____

• *Applications*
1. List an example to follow:

_____

2. Sin to avoid:

_____

3. Command to obey:

_____

4. Promise to claim:

_____

5. Prayer to echo:

_____

● *A Topical Study:* THE SECOND COMING OF CHRIST.[1]

> This same Jesus, which is taken up from you into heaven, shall so come in like manner (1:1).

The second coming of Christ is said to be mentioned 318 times in the 260 chapters of the New Testament, or once for every 25 verses. Paul preached much about Christ's return and frequently mentioned the subject in his epistles (e.g., 1 Thess. 1:10; 2:19; 3:13; 4:16-17; 5:1-4, 23). God bids us comfort one another with the reminder of the second coming of Christ (1 Thess. 4:18 context). This doctrine is not given the prominence in the church today that it received from Christ and the apostles. Paul emphasized three great truths concerning Christ:

(1) His death, (2) His resurrection, and (3) His coming again. These are His past, His present, and His future work for man. As Christians we need to look up for His return, and we also need to proclaim this promised event.

I. THE FACT OF CHRIST'S COMING

Why does a Christian believe that Christ is literally coming again? Because:

1. Jesus Himself said He would return (John 14:3).

2. The angels said He would (Acts 1:11), and they were not mistaken when they announced His first coming (Luke 1:30-33; Matt. 1:20-22).

3. The Holy Spirit, by the mouth of the apostles, repeatedly said He would (1 Thess. 4:16; Heb. 9:28; 10:37).

4. God, through the mouth of the prophets in the Old Testament said He would (Zech. 14:1, 3-4; Mal. 4:1-2).

II. THE MANNER OF CHRIST'S COMING

Christ's coming will be

1. personal, "the Lord himself" (1 Thess. 4:16).

2. bodily, "this same Jesus . . . in like manner" (Acts 1:11). Jesus went away with a real body, flesh and bones. He now sits at the right hand of God, ministering as our High Priest until the day when He will return for the church.

3. visibly, "every eye shall see him" (Rev. 1:7; cf. 1 John 3:2).

---

1. Recommended reading on this subject: René Pache, *The Return of Jesus Christ* (Chicago: Moody, 1955) and William K. Harrison, *Hope Triumphant* (Chicago: Moody, 1966).

4. suddenly, "as . . . lightning" (Matt. 24:27).
5. unexpectedly (Matt. 24:44, 37-39; Mark 13:35-36).
6. triumphantly (2 Thess. 1:7-10; Rev. 19:11-16).

III. THE OBJECT OF CHRIST'S COMING

Christ will come in order
1. to receive His own unto Himself—a phase of His coming called the rapture (1 Thess. 4:16-17; 1 Cor. 15:51-53).
2. to reward His servants (Matt. 16:27; Luke 19:11-27; 1 Cor. 9:25; 1 Thess. 2:19; 2 Tim. 4:8; 1 Peter 5:4; Rev. 3:21).
3. to judge and reign—a phase of Christ's second coming subsequent to the rapture (Rom. 14:12; 1 Cor. 3:13-15; 15:24-26; Matt. 25:32, 46; 2 Thess. 1:7-10; Jude 14-15; Zech. 14).

IV. THE TIME OF CHRIST'S COMING

The exact time of Christ's coming is not revealed (Matt. 24:36, 42; Mark 13:32; 1 Thess. 5:1-2). It has been hidden from us, with divine purpose. This makes the command of daily faithfulness a real test.

V. THE APPEAL TO CHRISTIANS IN VIEW OF CHRIST'S COMING

Make your own outline on the basis of these verses:
1. 1 Thessalonians 4:14

_____

2. Matthew 6:10; Revelation 22:20

_____

3. 2 Timothy 4:8

_____

4. 2 Timothy 4:1-2; Matthew 25:14-30; 28:18-20

_____

5. Mark 13:35; Romans 8:19, 23; 1 Thessalonians 5:6; Titus 2:13

_____

6. 1 Thessalonians 1:10; 2 Thessalonians 3:5

_____

7. 2 Peter 3:3-4

_____

8. Philippians 3:20; 1 John 3:1-3

9. 1 John 2:28

● *A Final Thought*
As you conclude this lesson, bring together these two statements
in your thinking and ponder their urgency:

> This Jesus . . . will come back.
> You will be witnesses for me.[2]

---

2. Acts 1:11 and 1:8 (*Good News for Modern Man*).

Lesson 3

The Holy Spirit Poured Forth

A cts 2 records a new experience in the history of God's people as connected with the Holy Spirit. In the design of God the day had arrived for an extended ministry of the third Person of the Trinity, the Holy Spirit, in the lives of believers. To this day, the Holy Spirit continues to serve thus.

On Chart C it is indicated that this was the time when the church was born. There had been an invisible organism of believers in Old Testament days and during Jesus' earthly ministry, but now the people of God—known as the church[1]—would be experiencing and serving in a new relationship to a more fully revealed God. This extended revelation was by the incarnate Christ (" God ... hath ... spoken ... by his Son," Heb. 1:1-2) and the indwelling Spirit (John 16:13-15). In light of this, it is accurate to say that the Pentecost day of Acts 2 was the birthday of the church.

• **Paragraph Divisions** At verses 1, 5, 14, 22, 37, 43. The chapter may be analyzed in two study segments: verses 1-21 and 22-47.

• **Observations and Questions**
1. Record the main subject of each paragraph, and arrive at a common theme which they all represent.
Verses 1-4—event:

_____

Verses 5-13—reaction:

_____

1. The first appearance of the word "church" in Acts is at 2:47 in some ancient manuscripts (Western family). In the other manuscripts its first appearance is at 5:11. A special study of the church is made in Lesson 4.

Verses 14-21—explanation:

_____

Verses 22-36—arraignment:

_____

Verses 37-42—response:

_____

Verses 43-47—results:

_____

A common theme:

_____

2. Of the Trinity, who is the prominent Person in verses 1-21?

_____

In verses 22-47?

_____

3. How is the ministry of the Spirit shown to magnify Jesus Christ (cf. 17*a* with 20*b*-21)?

_____

4. What was God's purpose in making the Holy Spirit's coming so dramatic?

_____

Compare those special manifestations of verses 1-4 with the things that transpire in verses 44-47, when the everyday routine of the Jerusalem church has begun to set in.

_____

What was *temporary* about the former and *permanent* about the latter?

_____

5. Compare these questions and their settings: "What meaneth this?" (v. 12) with "What shall we do?" (v. 37).

_____

6. Compare "Jesus...ye...crucified" (vv. 22-23) with "This Jesus ...God raised up" (v. 32).

_____

_____

7. What does this chapter teach about the way of salvation and the fellowship of believers?

_____

_____

8. What verse stands out to you as being a key verse in the chapter?

_____

_____

- **Applications**
1. example to follow:

_____

2. sin to avoid:

_____

3. command to obey:

_____

4. promise to claim:

_____

5. prayer to echo:

_____

- **A Topical Study** THE HOLY SPIRIT[2]

I will pour out of my spirit upon all flesh (3:17).

It is of the utmost importance that we know who or what the Holy Spirit is: whether the Holy Spirit is simply an *influence* emanating from God, a *power* that God imparts to us, or whether the Holy Spirit is a *person*. The Scriptures teach that the Holy Spirit is a divine Person, the third Person of the Trinity. He is not an influence that we are somehow to get hold of and use. Furthermore, the Scriptures teach that this divine Person, infinitely wise, holy

2. Recommended reading: René Pache, *The Person and Work of the Holy Spirit* (Chicago: Moody, 1954); Charles Ryrie, *The Holy Spirit* (Chicago: Moody, 1965).

and tender, was sent here from heaven on the day of Pentecost to take the place of the ascended Lord; and that He is in the world today, doing His appointed work. Does it not behoove us to search the Scriptures diligently and learn all we can about the Holy Spirit?

I. THE PERSONALITY OF THE HOLY SPIRIT

That the Holy Spirit is a Person is implied throughout the Scriptures. For example, personal characteristics are ascribed to Him: intellect (1 Cor. 12:11); emotion (Rom. 15:30); will (1 Cor. 12:11). But the doctrine of His personality is also expressly declared in such verses as John 14:16-17, 26; 15:26; 16:7-15. Notice the personal pronouns in these passages. Christ referred to the Holy Spirit not as "it" but as "He."

The Holy Spirit is a *divine* Person. He is one of the three Persons of the Trinity (read Matt. 28:19; 1 Cor. 12:4-6; 2 Cor. 13:14; Acts 5:3-4). Attributes of Deity are affirmed of Him (e.g., omnipotence, Luke 1:35); and works of Deity are ascribed to Him (e.g., regeneration, John 3:5).

II. THE WORKS OF THE HOLY SPIRIT

It amazes one to realize the large number of different works in which the Holy Spirit is engaged. As an exercise, record the work cited in each of the following passages:

John	14:26	_____
	15:26	_____
	16:8	_____
Acts	5:30-32	_____
	13:2-4	_____
	16:6-7	_____
Titus	3:5 (ASV)	
John	3:5	_____
1 Cor.	3:16	_____
	12:4-11	_____
Eph.	3:16	_____
	4:30	_____

	5:18	_____
Rom.	8:11	_____
	8:14	_____
	8:26	_____
Gal.	5:22-23	_____

III. THE INDWELLING OF THE HOLY SPIRIT

The Holy Spirit takes up His dwelling in the heart of the believer at the moment of regeneration (read John 14:17; 1 Cor. 6:19; Rom. 8:9). So *all* belivers are indwelt by the Spirit. Some believers are not aware of this blessed truth. Christians can suppress His activity by grieving Him (Eph. 4:30) and quenching Him (1 Thess. 5:19). He wants control of our whole being—spirit, soul, and body—but does not force this on anyone.

If we are children of God we are not so much to pray that the Spirit may come and dwell in us; for He does that already. We are rather to recognize His presence, His gracious and glorious indwelling, and give Him complete control of the house He already inhabits, and strive to so live as not to grieve this Holy one, this Divine guest.[3]

IV. THE FILLING OF THE HOLY SPIRIT

All believers are indwelt by the Spirit; not all believers are filled with the Spirit. The one conditional work of the Holy Spirit with respect to the Christian is that of filling. Every child of God is commanded to be filled with the Spirit. It should be the *normal* Christian relationship to the Spirit. "Be filled [literally, "be being filled"] with the Spirit" (Eph. 5:18*b*). The conditions for such day-to-day filling or control are:
1. a yielded will ("quench not," 1 Thess. 5:19)
2. confessed sin ("grieve not," Eph. 4:30)
3. faith and obedience ("walk by," Gal. 5:16)

All Christians should be Spirit-filled Christians, for this is God's will for His people. Do we recognize the Holy Spirit as a real, divine Person dwelling in us and wanting control over us each day of our lives?

3. R.A. Torrey, *What the Bible Teaches* (Westwood, N.J.: Revell, 1898), p. 250.

• *A Final Thought*

The closing verses of Acts 2 tell us that the early Christians dwelt together in a fellowship of love. Only the Holy Spirit in control of their hearts made this possible. Compare the familiar apostolic benediction: "The grace of the Lord Jesus Christ, and the love of God, and the *fellowship of the Holy Spirit* be with you all" (2 Cor. 13:13, *Berkeley*, italics added).

Lesson 4

A Miracle and a Sermon

Chapters 1-7 of Acts may be divided into two parts, dealing with the birth and infancy of the church. This is shown in Chart D.

BIRTH AND INFANCY   **Chart D**

CHURCH ESTABLISHED		
1 Church Is Born	3 Church Grows Through Testing	7

As of the end of chapter 2, the infant local church of believers in Jerusalem is basking in the sunlight of the fellowship of saints. The clouds of trial, however, were looming on the horizon. Endurance in the trials would mean growth for this church as well as for all others like it that would come into being in the years and centuries to come. The occasion for the first of these trials, arrest (chap. 4), is the story of Acts 3. It is the story of a miracle and a sermon.

• **Paragraph Divisions** At verses 1, 11, 19

• **Observations and Questions**
1. Which paragraphs record Peter's sermon?

_____

2. What main truth did Peter emphasize in performing the miracle (vv. 1-10)?

_____

_____

27

3. How did he interpret the miracle in his sermon (vv. 11-18)?

_____

_____

4. What was the main exhortation of his sermon (vv. 19-26)?

_____

_____

About God's Son Jesus?

_____

6. What is taught here about
salvation:

_____

judgment:

_____

Israel:

_____

- **Applications**
1. example to follow:

_____

2. sin to avoid:

_____

3. command to obey:

_____

4. promise to claim:

_____

- **A Topical Study** THE CHURCH

> The Lord added to the church daily (2:47).

I. THE WORD "CHURCH"

The English word "church" comes from the Greek *kuriakos* ("belonging to the Lord"), but in the New Testament it translates another Greek word, *ekklesiā* ("called-out ones").

Ekklesiā is essentially a post-Pentecost word. It appears a few times in the Greek translation (Septuagint) of the Old Testament, translated into English as "congregation."[1] It appears more than a hundred times in the New Testament, all but three distributed rather evenly from Acts to Revelation.[2]

II. THE NEW TESTAMENT CHURCH

When one compares the Old and New Testaments, many basic things remain the same. Examples of such unchanging truths are: the Giver of salvation (God); the way of salvation (by God's grace, through man's faith); the saved people (the redeemed of God). Everyone who will dwell with God in heaven will be there because his sins were atoned for by Jesus' blood.

Concerning some things, there is progression and development as one moves from the Old to the New Testament. For example, God has used different ways of revealing truth (read Heb. 1:1-2). The functioning of each of the Persons of the Trinity (called "economic Trinity") has varied from time to time. During His earthly ministry, Jesus served in a state of humiliation. Now He serves in a state of exaltation. The Holy Spirit ministers today in a fuller way than His service is described in the Old Testament.

In the Old Testament most of God's people are of the stock of Israel. In the New Testament, God's people are from all groups. For this and other reasons the new word "church" appears in the New Testament to represent this new constituency of God's family.

New Testament references to "church" are of three different kinds:

1. Invisible church—all believers, whether alive or dead, who are members of Christ's body (read Eph. 1:22-23; 5:23, 25-27). "Where Christ is, there is the Church."

2. Visible church at large—a constituency of all believers living at any one time (Acts 8:3; cf. "churches" in Acts 9:31).

3. Visible local church—a fellowship of believers who worship in a given locality (e.g., Antioch, Acts 13:1). It is possible for people to have their names on the membership roll of a church, and not be believers (cf. Rev. 2, 3).

II. THE FUNCTIONING CHURCH

The church is
1. for the praise of God's glory (Eph. 1:6; 2:7)
2. for the witness of truth (1 Tim. 3:15)

1. Stephen uses the word in Acts 7:38 to describe an Old Testament group.
2. The three appearances before Acts are in Matthew 16:18 and 18:17.

3. for the salvation of men (Mark 16:15; 1 Cor. 4:1; 2 Cor. 5:19).

IV. THE TRIUMPHANT CHURCH

The church in the world is sometimes referred to as the militant church because of its mandate to speak and act in a dark and evil society where Satan has been permitted to exercise much power. But one day when Christ comes it will rise as the triumphant church and enter into the rewards of victory (read Matt. 13:36-43; Rom. 8:18-23; 1 Thess. 4:14-17; Eph. 5:25-27; 1 John 3:2; Rev. 7:9 ff).

• *A Final Thought*
"You . . . *killed* the Prince of *life!*" (3:14-15, italics added) charged Peter. It is truly a contradiction for a man to reject Jesus Christ.

Lesson 5

The Test of Conviction

The hosts of darkness always react when the light of the gospel of God scans its beams in their direction. Some people run from the light; some try to destroy it; a few will surrender their wills and accept its revelation of saving grace. Acts 4 reports how false religionists reacted to the miracle and sermon of Peter and how the nucleus of believers around Peter and John resolved this problem triumphantly. This was a milestone in the early growth of the church.

● **Paragraph Divisions** At verses 1, 5, 13, 23, 32, 37

● **Observations and Questions**

1. There are many contrasts in this chapter. Observe the "how-beit" of verse 4. Contrast the first and last paragraphs.

_____

_____

2. Identify the main subject of each paragraph:
Verses 1-4—reaction:

_____

Verses 5-12—question and explanation:

_____

Verses 13-22—disposition:

_____

Verses 23-31—prayer:

_____

Verses 32-37—blessing:

_____

31

3. Locate a key verse in the chapter for each of these subjects:

salvation _____

Christian conviction _____

fruitful witness _____

4. What various ways is Jesus referred to in the chapter?

_____

_____

5. What lessons about boldness in witness are taught here?

_____

_____

6. What do you learn about prevailing prayer in verses 23-31?

_____

_____

_____

_____

- *Applications*
1. example to follow:

_____

2. sin to avoid:

_____

3. command to obey:

_____

4. promise to claim:

_____

5. prayer to echo:

_____

- *A Topical Study* THE NEW BIRTH

> Neither is there salvation in any other: for there is none other name under heaven given among men, whereby we must be saved (4:12).

This verse tells us that men are saved by Jesus Christ and by no one else. But what does it mean to be saved, and how is one saved?

32

Some people who answer yes to the question, Are you a Christian? are uncomfortable with the question, Have you been saved? This is because, for many, being a Christian is merely being a member of a church, living as a good neighbor, turning over a new leaf, or giving generously to noble causes. But Christians are "Christ ones"—those who have been regenerated by the Spirit of God and who have come into His fellowship as His children.

Every true believer in Christ—whether parent, Sunday school teacher, friend, layman, minister—should be able to explain to the unsaved how to become a Christian. The entire book of Romans dwells on the general subject of salvation. Verses from different books of the New Testament are brought together in the following outline, teaching various aspects of the doctrine of the new birth.

I. YOU MUST BE BORN AGAIN (John 3:3-7)

Note the passive form of the verb "be born." This is something that must be done *to* you or *for* you, not *by* you, although there is something that you must do in order to make the new birth possible for you.

II. WHY MUST ONE BE BORN AGAIN in order to enter the kingdom of God?

Romans 8:7-8 answers the question. By natural generation we are brought into this world and, if we so live after the flesh, we shall die in our sins (Rom. 8:13). It is impossible for the unsaved—the carnally minded—to enter God's kingdom and family when he is at "enmity against God," "not subject to the law of God," and utterly incapable of being subject to that law and of pleasing Him (Rom. 8:7-8). The natural, unregenerate man is blind to the things of the Spirit (1 Cor. 2:14) and corrupt in his affections (Gal. 5:19-21). This is his condition regardless of how cultured, refined, or outwardly moral he may be.

III. WHAT IS THE NEW BIRTH? (Read 2 Peter 1:4)

The new birth is the impartation of God's nature. Ezekiel 36:26-27, though spoken primarily to Israel, describes what takes place in every human life at the time of regeneration. "In the new birth God imparts to us His own wise and holy nature, a nature that thinks as God thinks, feels as God feels, wills as God wills."

IV. HOW CAN ONE BE BORN AGAIN?

What is man's part? What must I do? Read John 1:12-13. To be born again I must believe in Jesus Christ and receive Him into my heart as my Saviour. I must confess the Lord Jesus and believe in my heart that God raised Him from the dead (Rom. 10:9). This new life is by faith—"that believing ye might have life through his name" (John 20:31).

V. RESULTS OF THE NEW BIRTH

"Old things are passed away, behold, all things are become new" (2 Cor. 5:17b). When I receive Jesus Christ as my personal Saviour and am born of the Spirit, a new creation has taken place. From that time forth I am a temple of God, the Spirit of God dwelling in me (1 Cor. 3:16; 6:19), and the progressive process of being made anew into the likeness of my Creator begins.

VI. ASSURANCE OF THE NEW BIRTH

How may I know that this great miracle has taken place within me? In two ways. First, by God's Word. If I have done my part (believe and receive), God has done His part (read John 1:12). Second, I may know by my own experience, according to the following tests:

1. 1 John 5:1. Do I believe that Jesus is the Christ?
2. 1 John 5:4. Am I overcoming the world?
3. 1 John 3:9. "The person who has been born into God's family does not make a practice of sinning" (*Living Bible*). Am I practicing sin? Observe the present tense of the verb in this passage, denoting progressive or continued action. It is not taught that the one begotten of God never sins in a single act, but that he does not make a practice of sin.
4. 1 John 2:29. Am I practicing righteousness?
5. 1 John 4:7. Do I love all other Christians? The sense of the word "love" is "not mere emotion or sentiment, but that genuine desire for another's good that leads to sacrifice for him. . . . This love is the supreme result, evidence and test of the New Birth."[1]

• *A Final Thought*
The apostles' primary concern was not their physical safety or public reputation. It was that they might continue to speak the word of the gospel to people who needed to be saved.

1. R.A. Torrey, *What the Bible Teaches* (Westwood, N.J.: Revell, 1898), p. 332.

Lesson 6

More Test and Victories

Not all hindrances to the work of the church come from without the fellowship—some are from within. And sometimes these are the most disruptive ones. This is the story of the first part of Acts 5, introduced by the ominous word "but." Peter's undelayed diagnosis and disposition of the offense partly explains the victories of the Christian group in the remainder of the chapter.

• **Paragraph Divisions** At verses 1, 12, 17, 27, 33, 41

• **Observations and Questions**
   1. Following the paragraphical method of study, read the chapter and record the principal subject of each paragraph. Observe how verses 11, 16 and 41-42 describe the state and activity of the Jerusalem church during these days.
   2. Observe how the narrative unfolds tests followed by victories. Record these on Chart E.

TESTS AND VICTORIES   **Chart E**

TEST	VICTORY
5:1-11	5:12-16
5:17	5:19-26
5:27-28	5:29-32
5:33-40	5:41-42

3. Words and phrases to think about:
"lied unto . . . God" (v. 4)
"fear" (v. 11)
"shadow of Peter" (v. 15)
"worthy to suffer" (v. 41)
4. Apply these tremendous statements to today:

We ought to obey God rather than men (5:29).
If it be of God, ye cannot overthrow it (5:39).

• *Applications*
1. example to follow:

_____

2. sin to avoid:

_____

3. command to obey:

_____

4. promise to claim:

_____

• *A Topical Study* SATAN

Why hath Satan filled thine heart to lie to the Holy Ghost? (5:3).

Many Christians are not aware that the Bible has so much to say regarding Satan. The existence of a real, personal devil is doubted by many, and clear views as to his nature, power, work and destiny are held by comparatively few.

Satan is man's worst enemy. He is a fearful being, powerful, cunning, malignantly wicked, seeing constantly the ruin of souls and against whose devices we are warned in the strongest language throughout the Bible. Many things about the devil are not clearly revealed, for example, his origin and why his power is permitted. But we should diligently search out and ponder all that God has been pleased to tell us about our archenemy. "The secret things belong unto the Lord our God: but those things which are revealed belong unto us and to our children for ever" (Deut. 29:29). "The Bible doctrine regarding Satan is a very practical doctrine. There are certainly few doctrines that will go further than this in teaching us our utter dependence upon God and in driving us to prayer."[1]

1. R.A. Torrey, *What the Bible Teaches* (Westwood, N.J.: Revell, 1898), p. 513.

Below are listed some of the main facts about Satan, as taught by the Bible.

I. SATAN'S NAME AND TITLES

The Hebrew, Greek, and English names are all the same: Satan. The word means "adversary," which accurately identifies this enemy of God and man. Titles ascribed to him include: the devil (slanderer) (Matt. 4:1); accuser (Rev. 12:10); Beelzebub (Matt. 12:24); deceiver (Rev. 12:9); great dragon (Rev. 12:9); the wicked one (Matt. 13:19); father of lies (John 8:44); god of this world (2 Cor. 4:4); murderer (John 8:44); the old serpent (Rev. 12:9); prince of this world (John 12:31); prince of the power of the air (Eph. 2:2); tempter (Matt. 4:5).

II. SATAN'S EXISTENCE AS A PERSONALITY

That Satan is a being with personality is taught by many passages in both the Old and New Testaments. Compare the first reference to him, in Genesis 3:1, with the last, in Revelation 20:2, 10. The following activities assigned to him indicate he has personality:
acting (Job 2:7; Acts 5:3; John 13:27)
speaking (Job 1:9-11; Matt. 4:8-11)
moving (Job 1:7; 1 Peter 5:8)
suggesting (1 Chron. 21:1; John 13:2)
deceiving (Eph. 6:11; 2 Cor. 2:11)
tempting (Gen. 3:1-5; Matt. 4:8-11)
These things could only be done by a being with personality. The personality of Satan is just as real as the personality of Jesus Christ.

III. SATAN'S SPHERE OF ACTIVITY, POSITION, AND POWER

Satan moves in two realms. He is the head of the domain of evil spirits (Luke 11:14-18; Matt. 25:41), and he is lord over the world of lost humanity (Eph. 2:2; 1 John 5:19). He also is permitted to tempt, hinder and accuse the children of God (cf. 1 Pet. 5:8; Eph. 6:11-18; 1 Thess. 2:18). Though he has all this power, it is only as permitted by God, within bonds (cf. Job 1:12; 2:6; Luke 22:31).

Satan's chief method is deception (2 Cor. 11:3; Rev. 12:9), and his major purpose is to be worshiped (Matt. 4:9; 1 Cor. 10:20). He has under him beings so great in power and dignity as to be spoken of as principalities, powers, world rulers, spiritual hosts of wickedness in the heavenly places (see Eph. 6:11-12). Satan has vast power, far exceeding that of unaided man. The conflict we have on hand against Satan and his hosts is terrific. It is only in God's strength that we can hope to successfully meet him. In Jude 9 we see that even the archangel Michael did not dare to bring a railing accusation (judgment) against him.

IV. SATAN'S WICKEDNESS

This is seen in verses cited above, in addition to the following:

He "sinneth from the beginning" (1 John 3:8). Concerning his origin, John 8:44 implies that he is a fallen being (cf. 1 Tim. 3:6).

He was a murderer and liar from the beginning (John 8:44).

He blinds men's minds (2 Cor. 4:4).

He takes away the saving Word of God from men's hearts (Luke 8:12).

V. SATAN'S DOOM IS SURE

Throughout all of this world's history, Satan has been deceiving and trying to ruin mankind, but at Calvary his dominion received its deathblow. By Christ's death Satan's power was utterly undermined and doomed (Heb. 2:14, ASV*). Eternal fire is prepared for him and his angels (Matt. 25:41, ASV), and eventually he will be cast into that lake of fire together with all those who are not found written in the book of life (Rev. 20:10, 15; 21:8).

• *A Final Thought*

Satan today continues his attack on God's work, even as he did in the days of Acts. We who have been delivered from the power and kingdom of darkness (Col. 1:13) should be alert to the fact that he still is permitted to hurl his fiery darts against us. Ours is the promised victory, but we must heed the clear commands of God as given in these verses (read them): 1 Peter 5:8; Ephesians 4:27; 6:11; James 4:7.

*American Standard Version.

Stephen the Martyr

Before Paul was saved, there lived a man whose holy passion was accurately described by words later penned for Holy Writ by the apostle from Tarsus: "That in nothing I shall be ashamed, but that with all boldness, as always, so now also Christ shall be magnified in my body, whether it be by life, or by death" (Phil. 1:20). That man was Stephen.

This lesson covers those two chapters of Acts that tell the story of Stephen. In the first part of chapter 6, Stephen is one of a group of seven men. From 6:8 to the end of chapter 7, the narrative singles out Stephen, to tell of his unique and triumphant martyrdom.

- **Paragraph Divisions**
  Part I (in life): At verses 6:1, 7
  Part II (in death): 6:8, 7:2, 8*b*, 20, 30, 35, 44, 51, 54 (Stephen's message includes 7:2-50)

- **Observations and Questions**
  Stephen is usually remembered for his martyrdom. That was his ministry "by death" (Phil. 1:20). (Cf. Acts 22:20: "martyr" means witness.) We should also remember him, however, for his brief but faithful ministry "by life" as one of the seven deacons serving in the "business" phase of the Jerusalem church (see 6:2-3). This twofold story of Stephen is organized in Acts as illustrated in Chart F.

1. Study carefully the verses of Part I (6:1-7). Identify the problem suggested in verse 1 by the three words: multiplied, murmuring, ministration.

2. Compare the tasks of (1) serving tables and (2) serving the Word and prayer. Measure the importance of the former by the spiritual traits of Stephen, one of the seven chosen to serve in that capacity. Keep in mind that the deacons chosen to serve tables also ministered in word as well, as the stories of Stephen and Philip disclose.

_____

_____

STEPHEN'S LIFE AND DEATH   **Chart F**

		Ministry of Serving Tables	6:1-6
PART 1	By Life	Fruit of the Ministry	6:7
PART II	By Death	Ministry of Words and Miracles	6:8—8:1a
		Fruit of the Ministry	8:1b ff.

Record the different ways by which Stephen is identified and described in chapters 6 and 7.

_____

_____

3. Verse 7 records the fruit of the church described in verses 1-6. What is meant by the phrase "the word of God increased"?

_____

_____

Compare the readings of other versions.
4. Now read carefully the verses of Part II (6:8-8:1a). Record the main content of each of the following parts:
6:8-7:1

_____

7:2-50

_____

7:51-53

_____

5. You may want to spend extra time studying Stephen's defense (7:2-50). Was this a defense of himself or of the Christian gospel message?

Identify the main point of each paragraph (see paragraph divisions above). Why did Stephen choose to say so much about Israel's history? See 7:51*b*.

---

6. Why did Luke include the short sentence of 8:1*a* at this point in his story?

---

7. What important spiritual lessons are taught in 7:54-8:1*a*?

• *A Topical Study* STEPHEN[1]

Stephen, a man full of faith and of the Holy Ghost (6:5).

A very interesting and profitable method of Bible study is the biographical method. In the study of a character of the Bible you should read all that the Bible says about him and then ponder long over the material.[2] Try to realize the circumstances and con-

---

1. F.B. Meyer has written helpful studies of such Bible characters as Moses, Joshua, Elijah, and Paul. Some of his thoughts on Stephen are reflected in parts of this character study.
2. Things to look for in the Bible in making a character study are: (1) birth and parentage, (2) early life and training, (3) conversion and any subsequent experiences, (4) character, (5) ministry for God, (6) relationship to others, (7) death and eulogy, (8) why the Bible includes this person in its narrative. The Bible of course does not speak on all these subjects for every person.

ditions described. Think how things must have been in that day, until the life stands out before you clearly, and you feel really acquainted with the one about whom you have been reading. In the case of Stephen, just about all we know about him is recorded in Acts 6 and 7. The facts given of his life are very few but impressive.

God has different ways of introducing to the world's notice His great servants. In some cases their lives rise gradually before us from the dawn of childhood to the zenith of their power and usefulness, and then as gradually sink softly to their close. In such a way is given to us the history of Jacob, Joseph, Moses, David, and others. We catch only a fleeting glimpse, and it is gone. Sometimes a hitherto unknown character appears suddenly, bursting in with a message from God and almost immediately disappearing. Elijah, John the Baptist, and Stephen are among these. We know absolutely nothing of Stephen's parents, home, birthplace, early surroundings, education. We have the story of only the last of his life, in particular the last day of his life.

All seven of the deacons appointed in chapter 6 were filled with the Holy Spirit, but Stephen seems to have been the spiritual giant of them all. Three times in this short record is this fullness of the Spirit mentioned concerning him.

Stephen was not content to confine himself to the business affairs of the church but took every possible opportunity to speak the truth and work for the spread of the gospel. When a delegation of Jews, who refused to believe that the crucified Carpenter of Galilee could be the long-expected Messiah, came to dispute the question with the believers, it was Stephen who met them with arguments of such convincing wisdom and power that they were unable to resist him. Oh, how they hated him for it! Realizing that if they convicted him at all it must be by fraud, they caught him, dragged him before the Sanhedrin, and set up false witnesses.

In answer to the high priest's stern question, "Are these things so?" (7:1) Stephen made a wonderful speech (chap. 7). Briefly he told the story of the nation's history, pointing out that all their great leaders had first been rejected by the men of their own day but afterward proved to be the deliverers whom God had chosen and sent. He cited the instance of Joseph (7:9-17), who was first rejected and sold by his brethren but was afterward raised to such great power that they had to acknowledge him as the savior of their lives (read Gen. 45:4-8; cf. Acts 7:9-17). Moses was also first rejected by the people, but he afterward delivered them from bondage and death in Egypt (7:20-36). The prophets were all rejected, persecuted, and slain by the men of their own day, but afterward were seen to be God's messengers (7:52-53). Stephen ended his speech by saying, in substance: "You people of this day are just like your ancestors; you always resist the Holy Spirit. Only you are worse than your fathers; they killed God's messengers who prophesied of the Messiah, but you have killed the Messiah Himself!" (Acts 7:51-53, paraphrase).

At such a charge the hatred of the people broke all bounds. They ran at Stephen and dragged him out of the city, threw off their coats, and stoned him to death. But Stephen was not crushed in mind and heart by the cruel blows that crashed against the body. With his face turned heavenward he was beholding the glories of the other world. God had drawn back the curtain of heaven, and Stephen was having a glimpse inside. In ecstasy he cried out: "Behold, I see the heavens opened, and the Son of man standing on the right hand of God" (Acts 7:56). Jesus was standing with outstretched arms to receive His faithful servant. With a prayer upon his lips for those sin-blinded ones who were murdering him, he fell asleep amid a shower of stones, and when he awoke he was in the presence of Jesus Christ.

As young Saul stood with those coats piled at his feet (7:58), he listened to Stephen's words and saw Stephen die. So deep an impression was made upon him that it was never effaced. Years afterward, Saul himself was on trial before that very Sanhedrin and for the very cause for which Stephen died. He, too, made great speeches, molded by much the same plan as that of the never to be forgotten address that he had heard Stephen make.

Stephen died for Christ after making one brief speech, but he helped to bring to Christ the man Paul, who for more than a quarter of a century spoke and wrote in burning words that have stirred and thrilled the church for nearly two thousand years, and who did more for the furthering of Christ's kingdom than perhaps any other man who ever lived.

• Summary of chapters 1-7

Before moving on to the next main section of Acts, review the first seven chapters, recalling the highlights of the story of the church's birth and infant years. Account for the various successes of the church despite the tremendous opposition and hindrances.

Lesson 8

Philip the Soul-Winner

With this lesson we reach the first main junction of Acts, a milestone in early church history. At 8:1*b*, with a "great persecution" setting in, the church was "scattered abroad throughout the regions of Judea and Samaria." Review Chart C, of which Chart G is an excerpt.

THE EARLY CHURCH   **Chart G**

1:1	8:1b	13:1 28:31
Jerusalem	Judea and Samaria	Uttermost Parts
Church Established	Church Scattered	Church Extended

The great persecution did not hinder the church. Rather, it helped its growth. The blood of those who gave their lives in martyrdom, like Stephen, was truly the "seed of the church" planted in the soil of heathen lands. The story of this lesson shows how the gospel did its work in the hearts of people living and visiting in Judea and Samaria.

Philip is the key person of chapter 8. Chapters 6-8 thus have a close relationship to each other, in that chapter 6 records the appointment of the Jerusalem church's seven deacons; chapter 7 tells the story of one of these, Stephen, who was privileged to die as a witness (martyr) for Christ; and chapter 8 describes the experiences of another of the seven, Philip, who was privileged to serve on as a living witness for Christ, leading souls to Him.

• **Paragraph Divisions** At verses 1, 4, 9, 14, 25, 26, 36

		8:1b	
	Scattering of the Church		

		4	
	Philip in Samaria		
		9	

		14	
	Special Mission of the Church		
		25	

		26	
	Philip and the Ethiopian		
		36	
		40	

45

• Observations and Questions

This is a chapter of many wonderful phrases concerning God's message, ministries, men, and methods. After you have read through the chapter a couple of times, underlining key phrases as you read, record these and other observations in the rectangle in Chart H. Note the general outline that is already shown. After you have recorded your observations, answer the following questions:

1. Observe how the positive note of verse 4 makes a bright commentary of verses 1-3.

2. What was the problem of verses 14-17?

_____

_____

Note that Peter and John, leaders of the church, were the official representatives present when the new Christians were identified with the larger fellowship of the church. You may want to refer to a commentary for help on this question of the receiving of the Holy Spirit.[1]

3. List the things taught by the chapter about God's

men

_____

message

_____

ministries

_____

methods

_____

4. What does the chapter teach about how to be saved, and about the fruits of salvation?

_____

_____

_____

_____

1. Cf. John F. Walvoord, *The Holy Spirit* (Grand Rapids: Zondervan, 1958), pp. 153-54.

• **Applications**
1. example to follow:

_____

2. sin to avoid:

_____

3. command to obey:

_____

4. promise to claim:

_____

• **A Topical Study** PERSONAL WORK IN SOUL-WINNING

Go near, and join thyself to this chariot (Acts 8:29*b*).

One reason the early church increased so rapidly was that each individual member felt his personal responsibility to share God's message with lost souls (cf. 8:1, 4).

I. EVERY CHRISTIAN'S RESPONSIBILITY

Most Christians today have referred the task of evangelism (telling the "glad tidings") to such "professional" servants as pastors and evangelists. But an honest view of Christian responsibility sees that every Christian should have some part in the ministry of winning souls to Jesus. Such a view is supported by these three purposes of soul-winning:

1. For Jesus' sake. The one great purpose for which Christ left heaven, lived, worked, suffered, prayed and died was soul-winning (Luke 19:10). If we are followers of His, that should be our purpose also. If we want to bring joy to the heart of Jesus, honor to His blessed name, and hasten the coming of His kingdom, one way to do it is to attract souls to Him.

2. For the sake of others. If we want to really benefit humanity, do real good to others, we must point them to Christ. Souls are perishing all around us, dying of the deadly disease of sin, without God and without hope (cf. Eph. 2:12). We know the only remedy for sin. Our duty is to urge lost souls to apply the remedy by accepting Christ.

3. For our own sake. The compulsion is twofold: because of the condemnation that is ours if we do not warn sinners (Ezek. 33:8) and because of the rich reward that is ours if we do win souls (Prov. 11:30; Dan. 12:3).

II. THE EXAMPLE OF PHILIP

Philip was a model soul-winner, but many of the qualifications he possessed were those that any one of us may possess. Notice a few points about Philip as a soul-winner:

1. Philip was a layman, serving as a deacon. He was not an ordained clergyman, nor one of the twelve apostles. And yet he was used of God in a mighty way.

2. Philip has an intense love for souls, which is necessary for Christian witness. Love for souls is not natural to the human heart, but God can give it to any one. How can one get a love for souls? Pray for such a love, and meditate on the worth of a human soul and the fearful condition of the lost. A soul is worth the price God paid for it (John 3:16).

3. Philip was in communion with God and was under the guidance of the Spirit. He talked with God and knew when God spoke to him (8:26). This is of great importance in soul-winning. We must constantly ask God's guidance as to where to go, to whom to speak, when to speak, what to say, and other similar questions.

4. Philip was obedient. He was doing great work in Samaria (see vv. 5-8). To human eyes it may have appeared more important to stay there, yet when God ordered him to move to the desert, he instantly obeyed (see v. 26-27).

5. Philip was a man taught in the Word of God. The Ethiopian could not understand the words he read. The natural man, who is not born again, needs help to understand the Scriptures (1 Cor. 2:14). Philip was able to take the Scriptures and show the Ethiopian the way of salvation (see v. 35). Can we do that? Can we sit down beside a seeking soul and show him from the Bible how to be saved, show him verses that tell what he must do to be saved? Every Christian ought to be prepared to do that.[2]

6. Last, but not least, Philip was a Spirit-filled man (Acts 6:3-8). The Spirit had full control of him. This is the supreme condition of successful soul-winning.

• *A Final Thought*

C.H. Spurgeon has suggested what he believed are the important qualifications for soul-winning, as to the Godward and

---

2. There are many good books on personal soul-winning that give this kind of practical help. For example, J.C. Macaulay and Robert H. Belton, *Personal Evangelism* (Chicago: Moody, 1956); Stephen F. Olford, *The Secret of Soul-Winning* (Chicago: Moody, 1963).

manward relationships.[3] As you conclude your study of this lesson, ponder over each of the following qualifications and measure your own life by them:

Godward	Manward
holiness of character	knowledge
spiritual life	sincerity
humility	evident earnestness
living faith	love
earnestness	unselfishness
simplicity of heart	seriousness
complete surrender	tenderness

3. C.H. Spurgeon, *The Soul-Winner* (Grand Rapids: Eerdmans, 1963, reprint), pp. 39, 65.

Conversion of Saul

One of the leaders of the cruel persecution was Saul of Tarsus, an intelligent, religious man. He was suffering severe pangs of conscience as he continued to follow the beckonings of Satan while the Lord was speaking to his heart (cf. 9:5). The narrative of Acts 9 contains one of the most striking contrasts in the entire Bible: the powerful murderous persecutor fighting Jesus becomes the impotent subdued servant proclaiming His praises. Truly a miracle transcending all description!

- **Paragraph Divisions** At verses 1, 10, 17, 19*b*, 26, 31

- **Observations and Questions**
1. Record the main point of each paragraph

_____

_____

_____

2. How does verse 31 serve the chapter?

_____

Compare this verse with 8:1-3.

_____

3. There are two views as to when Saul was saved: (1) at 9:1-9 or (2) at 9:18-19. What do you think? Justify your answer.

_____

_____

4. Observe the various references to Saul's preaching. What was the message he preached?

_____

5. Account for the disciples' hesitation in receiving Saul into their fellowship.

_____

6. List the various miracles of this chapter.

_____

_____

_____

7. What is taught about Christ here?

_____

_____

About divine call to service?

_____

_____

• *Applications*
1. example to follow:

_____

2. sin to avoid:

_____

3. command to obey:

_____

4. promise to claim:

_____

5. prayer to echo:

_____

• *A Topical Study* THE DEITY OF JESUS CHRIST

He preached Christ . . . that he is the Son of God (Acts 9:20).

The main truth that Paul emphasized as he preached in the synagogues of Damascus immediately following his conversion was that Christ was the Son of God (Acts 9:20). In his role as persecutor, Paul was not anti-God. In fact, he thought he was pleasing

God by persecuting the Christians. Then, fresh from the vision that showed him who Jesus really was (Acts 9:5), he wanted to retrace his steps, as it were, and tell the people, whom he had radically misinformed, who Jesus really was.

Many people today say they believe in the *divinity* of Christ but not in His *deity*, meaning that they believe Him to be Godlike, proceeding from God, but not that He is God. The Bible plainly teaches that Jesus Christ is God. It teaches this by direct statement (e.g., John 1:1-2, 14) and by attributing to Christ divine names, attributes, and offices that belong only to God. A few of these are as follows (read all the passages cited):

I. DIVINE NAMES

1. Mighty God, everlasting Father, Prince of peace (Isa. 9:6)
2. Immanuel ("God with us," Matt. 1:23)
3. Lord (Matt. 7:21-22; Luke 1:43; 2:11; John 20:28; Acts 16:31; 1 Cor. 12:3; Phil. 2:11)
4. Son of God (John 5:21-26; 10:36)
5. God (John 1:1; 20:28; Titus 2:13; Heb. 1:8; 2 Pet. 1:1; cf. 1 Tim. 3:15-16)
6. Alpha and Omega (Rev. 1:8, 17; 22:13)
7. Logos (John 1:1-5, 9-14; Rev. 19:13)

II. DIVINE ATTRIBUTES

1. Eternal (John 1:1-3; 8:58; Col. 1:16-17; Heb. 1:8-12; 7:3; 13:8; Rev. 1:8; 22:13)
2. Self-existent (John 1:4; 5:26-27; 10:30; 14:10; Phil. 2:6)
3. Holy (Luke 1:35; John 8:36; Acts 3:14; 4:27; 2 Cor. 5:21; Heb. 4:15; 7:26)
4. Omnipotent (all-powerful); power over disease (Luke 4:39); death (Luke 7:14-15); nature (Matt. 8:26-27); demons (Luke 4:35-36, 41). (Read also Matt. 28:18; Mark 1:27; John 5:19-21; 1 Pet. 3:21-22; Heb. 1:8.)
5. Omniscient (all-wise) (Matt. 9:4; 12:25; Luke 5:22; 22:10-12; John 2:24-25; 4:16-19; 16:30; Col. 2:3)
6. Omnipresent (present everywhere) (Matt. 28:20; John 1:48; 3:13)
7. Of perfect love (Mark 10:21; Luke 23:34; John 10:11; 14:31; 15:13; Rom. 5:8; 8:37-39; Eph. 3:19)
8. Unchangeable (Heb. 1:10-12; 13:8)

III. DIVINE OFFICES

    1. Creator (John 1:3, 10; Eph. 3:9; Col. 1:16-18; Heb. 1:2, 10)
    2. Preserver (Col. 1:17; Heb. 1:3)
    3. Forgiver of sins (Matt. 9:2; Mark 2:5-10; Luke 5:20-24; 7:48)
    4. Conqueror of death (John 6:39, 44; 11:25)
    5. Judge (Matt. 13:39-43; John 5:22-23; Acts 10:42; 2 Cor. 5:10; 2 Tim. 4:1)

● *A Final Thought*
    Think over the ways in which the conditions named in Acts 9:31 are evidences of a healthy church:
    rest
    edification
    fear of the Lord
    comfort of the Holy Spirit
    multiplication

The Gospel for Gentiles

Up to this time in the brief history of the church, most of those who believed were Jewish. This is understandable, since the gospel was the fulfillment of the Jews' Scriptures. Jesus and His disciples were Jews, and His mission was primarily to the house of Israel. The disciples were thus now taking it for granted that the gospel was mainly for Jews, with Gentiles brought into the fellowship of the church only via the Jewish institutions. The time had now come for God to make clear that the gospel was for Gentile as well as Jew. Peter, leader of the church at this time, was the logical one to whom God would give such instruction. How God did this is the story of most of the passage under study now.

• **Paragraph Divisions** At verses 9:32, 36; 10:1, 9, 17, 23*b*, 34, 44, 48; 11:1

• **Observations and Questions**
1. Identify the main point of each paragraph, and then outline the segment.
2. What are Peter's experiences in 9:32-43?

_____

_____

_____

How will these prepare him for the events of chapter 10?

_____

_____

3. Who is the key person of this passage?

_____

Where was Paul at this time (see 9:30)?

4. Observe how devout a man Cornelius was (10:2). Was he a saved man before he heard Peter preach?

5. What is taught about Jesus and the way of salvation in 10:34-43?

6. Verse 44 speaks of Cornelius's company as hearing the Word. Did they *believe?* Read 11:1, 17-18 for your answer.

7. Apply 10:34 to today.

• *Applications*
1. example to follow:

2. sin to avoid:

3. command to obey:

4. promise to claim:

5. prayer to echo:

• *A Topical Study* GENTILES

> Then hath God also to the Gentiles granted repentance unto life (11:18).

In the book of Acts we are constantly hearing about Gentiles. Who are they? What does the Bible teach about them? Why is so much importance assigned them?

By definition, Gentiles are non-Jewish people—that is, people not descended from Abraham. In the Bible other words are sometimes used for non-Jewish people, such as "heathen," "people," "nations," and "Greeks."

Up to chapter 12 of Genesis there is no distinction between Jews and Gentiles. The term "children of men" was then used to refer to the entire human race (e.g., Gen. 11:5). With Abraham a new and great nation was made by God (Gen. 12:2), to be known throughout the ages by such names as "Israelites" (Ex. 9:7) and "Jews" (2 Kings 16:6).

From Genesis 12 on, the Old Testament has Israel primarily in view—a small but significant stream running from the vast river of the human race. For most of the New Testament after the gospels, Gentiles are the prominent group. The chronological sequence is: (1) children of men, (2) Israel, (3) Gentiles:

1. *Children of men.* World government and leadership was the responsibility of the whole human race. These were the years before the call of Abraham. The children of men failed to honor and obey God, bringing such judgments upon the world as a flood and confusion of tongues (Gen. 7-8; 11).

2. *Israel.* The nation Israel was begotten of Abraham around 2000 B.C. God offered to make Israel the ruling nation of the world, a source of blessing for all others (Gen. 12:2-3). The condition imposed was faithfulness and obedience to God. God was long-suffering in granting Israel many opportunities to prove their loyalty and first love. For their rejection of Him, captivities came in 722 B.C. and 586 B.C. with a worldwide dispersion of the remnants in A.D. 70.

3. *Gentiles.* When Israel forfeited its prominent place above all nations, God transferred the supremacy to Gentile nations. The condition was the same as that required of Israel: obedience to God. Would the Gentile nations recognize God as the supreme Ruler? World supremacy was first offered to Babylon (Dan. 2:36-39). When Babylon failed to meet the condition and bow in obedience to God, God passed the power on to the Medes and Persians. When they failed, He gave it to the Greeks; and when they failed, it passed to the Romans. The succession has continued to the present-day, with non-Jewish nations always involved. Israel is not in the picture as such, for Israel is a scattered nation. These are the "times of the Gentiles" (Luke 21:24).

Gentile supremacy will end in the last times (Dan. 2:44), God's judgment falling upon the world at the time of the second coming of Christ. The divine purpose in this present age is to take out from among the Gentiles a people for His name, the church, which is composed more largely of Gentiles than of Jews (see Acts

15:13-17). "The fulness of the Gentiles" mentioned in Romans 11:25 is the completion of this purpose of God in this age. When that time has come for the Gentiles, God will restore the promised kingdom to Israel (see Rom. 11).

● *A Final Thought*

God is no respecter of persons. This is supremely demonstrated in His gift offered to everyone: "For God loved the world so much that he gave his only Son, so that everyone who believes in him may not die but have eternal life" (John 3:16, *Good News for Modern Man*). This gospel is for Jew and Gentile alike.

Lesson 11

Acts 11:19–12:25

Antioch Christians

Before Luke recorded the church's first overseas mission, he told of its spiritual health and strength. The church then (beginning at chap. 13) was only about fifteen years old, and yet it was mature in many ways beyond its years. It was advancing geographically (in this lesson to Antioch), and it was growing stronger at the "home" church of Jerusalem, the saints there being involved in service, persecution, and prayer.

Although the Antioch church played a major role in only the first part of this study segment, it is the principal subject, because here is furnished the setting for the missionary venture of the following chapters. Study the map on Chart A, noting especially the location of Antioch with respect to Jerusalem.

There are two parts to the text of this lesson, shown in Chart I. Keep the chart's outline in mind as you study this lesson.

THE TAUGHT AND TESTED CHURCH   **Chart I**

11:19 The Taught Church	12:1 The Tested Church 12:25
Ministries in Antioch	Persecution in Jerusalem
Barnabas with Saul	Herod vs. Peter

• **Paragraph Divisions** At verses 11:19, 22, 27; 12:1, 7, 12, 18, 20, 24

• **Observations and Questions**
1. Note the references to Jews (11:19) and Gentiles ("Grecians," 11:20). Was the church putting into practice its new conviction concerning the universality of the gospel? _____

58

2. What are the signs of spiritual health in the Antioch church (11:19-30)?

_____

_____

3. Observe how Saul is brought into the story of Acts at 11:25. What do you suppose Saul had been doing at Tarsus?

_____

4. Compare what the Jerusalem church sent to Antioch (11:22) with what the Antioch church sent to Jerusalem (11:29). What was the common spirit?

_____

5. We tend to use the word "Christian" (11:26) rather freely. What are the implications and significances of such a title being applied to a believer?

_____

_____

6. What does 12:1-25 teach about prayer?

_____

7. Compare 12:2-23 with the concluding verse 24.

_____

_____

• *Applications*
1. example to follow:

_____

2. sin to avoid:

_____

3. command to obey:

_____

4. promise to claim:

_____

5. prayer to echo:

_____

• *A Topical Study* ANGELS

> [Peter] wist not that it was true which was done by the angels (12:9).
> It is his angel (12:15).

Throughout the book of Acts, as well as in many other parts of the Bible, there are frequent references to angels. Many people, however, have very vague or erroneous ideas about angels. Angels are an entirely different order of created beings from man. Believers in Christ are saints but are not and never will be angels. The blessedness of saints is far greater than any experience of angels.

The word translated "angel" means literally "messenger," a word suggesting one of the angels' major functions. The following outline describes some important truths that the Bible teaches about these created beings (read all the verses cited):

I. THE NATURE OF ANGELS

1. Angels are spirits (Heb. 1:13-14; Ps. 104:4), created by God (Neh. 9:6; Col. 1:16) before the creation of man (Job 38:7).
2. Though angels do not have bodies, they have revealed themselves in bodily form to men, conversing with them (Matt. 1:20; John 20:12-13; Acts 7:30; 12:7-8).
3. They are exceedingly numerous, constituting a company, not a race (Matt. 26:53; Heb. 12:22; Rev. 5:11; Luke 20:34-36).
4. They have great power and intelligence (Matt. 28:2, 4; Acts 5:19; 12:7, 23; 2 Pet. 2:11; Rev. 20:1-3; 2 Sam. 24:15-16; 2 Kings 19:35; Ps. 103:20).
5. They are glorious beings (Matt. 28:2-3; Rev. 10:1).
6. They do not marry or die (Matt. 22:30; Luke 20:35-36).
7. They are not to be worshiped (Col. 2:18; Rev. 22:8-9).
8. There are good angels and evil angels. Satan was the first of the angels to rebel against his Creator (cf. Luke 10:18 and Rev. 12:7-9 with Ezek. 28:12-19; Isa. 14:12-15). Of the evil angels that followed his example, some are not imprisoned in Tartarus (2 Pet. 2:4; Jude 6); others are free to support their leader, Satan, in his work (Matt. 25:41; Rom. 8:38; 1 Cor. 6:3; Eph. 1:21; 6:12; Col. 2:15; Rev. 9:14). Demons would also be classified as evil spirits permit-

ted the freedom to serve their leader (Matt. 8:16; 10:1, 8; Luke 10:17, 20). The ultimate destiny of Satan and his angels is everlasting fire (Matt. 25:41; Rev. 20:10).

II. THE MINISTRY OF HOLY ANGELS

1. They praise and worship God and His Son Jesus (Ps. 103:20; 148:2; Luke 2:13; Heb. 1:6; Rev. 5:11).
2. They execute God's judgments and purposes (Num. 22:22; Matt. 13:41; Acts 12:23). They have special functions at important junctions of world history. For example, angels were used to give the law to Israel on Mount Sinai (Gal. 3:19). A multitude of angels sang praises to God on the birth of the Child Jesus (Luke 2:13-14). An angel served in connection with the vision of the gospel to Gentiles (Acts 10:3). And angels will serve in special capacities in the events of the last days (e.g., 2 Thess. 1:7).
3. They minister to God's people in guiding, protecting, and strengthening (Gen. 19:11; 1 Kings 19:5-7; Ps. 34:7; 91:11; Dan. 3:28; 6:22; Matt. 4:11; 18:10; Acts 5:19; 12:7-10; Heb. 1:14). Note their ministry to Jesus (e.g., Matt. 4:11).
4. They will accompany Christ at His final appearances in the history of this world, for example, at the rapture (1 Thess. 4:16) and the last judgment (Matt. 25:31; 2 Thess. 1:7). They will continue to serve Him for eternity (cf. Rev. 21:12).

How inconceivably glorious will that day be when innumerable hosts like the shining ones described in Revelation 10:1 and Matthew 28:2-3 shall suddenly appear together with Christ, who outshines them all as the sun outshines a tallow candle, coming in the clouds of heaven to this earth. This is no fancy but a literal fact that shall take place one day. Those who are ashamed to confess their faith in Christ and His Word should note what is said of them in Mark 8:38.

• A Final Thought

> Prayer for him was being made fervently by the church to God (Acts 12:5).

We are so dependent on God for *everything* that the breath of prayer should be as indispensable as the breath of our lungs. It could be that our prayer life has waned because we are not really conscious of our dependency on God.

Lesson 12

Acts 13:1–14:28

First Missionary Journey

Paul's first missionary journey was the first organized effort to go overseas with the gospel. World evangelization was of course the plan that Jesus shared with His apostles (1:8). Now it was the time to execute such a plan. We observe from the text that it was not Paul, nor the church, but the Holy Spirit who took the initiative of this new venture (13:2). It was God's plan, and it was God's work. The missionaries were to be His instruments in the work (cf. 14:26-27).

Evangelization of the world—home and foreign missions—is the greatest enterprise of God in this age. The book of Acts is not only a history of the church's first thirty years of missions. It also serves as a valuable commentary and handbook on missions, dealing with basic fundamentals and answering important questions about the subject. Look for these as you study the next eight or so chapters of Acts, which report the highlights of Paul's three missionary journeys. (Study the map on Chart A to become acquainted with the places Paul visited on his first journey.)

HISTORY OF MISSIONS Chart J

A.D. 47	Church Extends Overseas		A.D. 56
1st Journey	Jerusalem Council	2d Journey	3d Journey
13:1	15:1	15:36	18:23 21:17

62

- *Main Divisions* The opening verse of each new division in the first journey is identified in the following outline:
    Commission—13:1
    Island tour—13:4
    Inland tour—Antioch, 13:14
    —Iconium, 14:1
    —Lystra and Derbe, 14:6
    Return tour—14:21
    Homecoming—14;26

- *Observations and Questions*
1. Read the passage first to see the highlights of the journey. Underline important words and phrases in your Bible.
2. What was the main ministry of Paul[1] in each place he visited? Observe how fruitful his ministry was.

---

3. What was the Holy Spirit's purpose in planting the gospel in the large cities?

---

4. Observe how quickly churches were organized in the cities where Paul preached (see 14:21-23).
5. Observe the occasions of opposition and how Paul reacted in each case.
6. Observe the variety of audiences and situations of Paul's ministry. Paul preached to all classes of people—Jew and Gentile, educated and superstitious, receptive and antagonistic, rich and poor. He always adapted his manner of presenting the gospel to the capacity of his hearers, but the truth was always the same, the Word of God. Paul always preached the pure gospel.
7. Observe Paul's reference to justification in 13:39. Justification by faith was one of Paul's greatest themes in his epistles (see Rom. 3:24, 28; 4:2; 5:1, 9; Gal. 2:16; 3:8). Here are some definitions and descriptions of justification: Justification is the judicial act of God whereby He justly declares righteous the one who believes in Jesus Christ. A man is justified before God when God reckons or declares him to be righteous.
    The justified believer has been in court and has been cleared.
    When we are justified we stand before God, not only forgiven of sin, but as if we never had sinned (cf. 13:38).
    Faith in Jesus is the only condition on which men are justified.

1. Note that the name Paul replaces the Hebrew name Saul at 13:9. For the rest of Acts Luke uses the name Paul. Paul apparently had both names from youth, Saul being the Hebraic form.

We are justified by faith without works, but we are not justified by a faith that is without works. The faith that saves is the faith that leads to works.

8. Compare the commissioning before the journey (13:3) and the report after the journey (14:27).

• *Applications*

1. example to follow:

---

2. sin to avoid:

---

3. command to obey:

---

4. promise to claim:

---

5. prayer to echo:

• *A Topical Study* PRAYER

> And when they had fasted and prayed . . . they sent them away (13:3).

Prayer plays an important part in this story. The Antioch church prayed for the missionaries (13:3), and the missionaries prayed for the newly organized churches (14:23). Throughout the book of Acts, indeed throughout the entire Bible, we see great things brought about by prayer. Many Christians in practice doubt the efficacy of prayer because to them prayer is more a habit than it is a force. They pray as a religious duty and not as a means to an end. The Bible clearly teaches that God means our prayers to have an answer, so if our prayers are not being answered it is because we are not praying aright. Someone has said, "There is nothing we more need to study and practice than the art of praying aright. The powers of the eternal world are placed at the disposal of believing prayer." It is a great thing to know how to speak to men so as to move them to action, but it is a greater thing to know how to speak to God and watch Him respond.

God has given promises regarding prayer that are staggering because they are so great. See, for example, John 14:14-15; 16:23.

But notice the conditions that must be fulfilled before we can claim such promises. Here are seven conditions, among others, of answered prayer:

1. *Forsaken sin* (Ps. 66:18). Herein lies a very simple explanation why many of us pray and are not heard. In our heart we must abhor sin. Read Psalm 51 to learn what contriteness for sin is.

2. *A forgiving spirit* (Mark 11:25-26). Many fail to receive answers to prayer because they have an unforgiving spirit toward someone.

3. *A spiritual motive* (James 4:3). The chief motive in prayer should be that God may be glorified in the answer, not that we may be gratified or benefited. Thousands of requests, perfectly proper in themselves, remain ungranted because the motive is selfish.

4. *Obedience* (1 John 3:22). "Here we find one of the greatest secrets of prevailing prayer. If we listen to God's commandments God will listen to our prayers. If we do as He bids us in His Word, He will do as we ask Him in our prayers. If we do what pleases Him, He will do what pleases us."[2]

5. *Faith* (Mark 11:24; Matt. 21:22). This is not general faith in God or Christ but a specific faith that the very things we are asking, will be given. We are to have an unwavering expectation of answered prayer.

6. *Praying according to God's will* (1 John 5:14). The question here is, of course, how to know God's will. God withholds many things from us, but that which may be known of His will is learned through knowing *Him* and the way He works more intimately. This comes by spiritual eyes and ears that are alert to what He discloses in (1) the Bible, (2) circumstances, and (3) the still small voice of His Spirit. Knowing that we can and do pray amiss at times concerning God's will, we should always have the attitude of heart that says, "Thy will, not mine, be done." Such a heart readily accepts answers from God like "No" and "Wait."

7. *Praying in Jesus' name* (John 16:23). All blessings come to us through Jesus Christ. Torrey uses the illustration of a check drawn on a bank. A check made out to me is good for the amount written if the payer has that much money in the bank. It matters not whether or not I have any money in my own bank account. "Jesus Christ has given to believers in Him the right to put His name upon their checks. We have nothing in the bank of heaven, no claim upon it. He has unlimited credit there."[3]

2. R.A. Torrey, *What the Bible Teaches* (Westwood, N.J.: Revell, 1898), p. 411.
3. Ibid, p. 446.

Only glimpses of this great importance of prayer could the apostles get before Pentecost. But the Spirit coming and filling at Pentecost elevated prayer to its vital and all-commanding position in the Gospel of Christ. The call now of prayer to every saint is the Spirit's loudest and most exigent call. Sainthood's piety is made, refined, perfected, by prayer. The Gospel moves with slow and timid pace when the saints are not at their prayers early and late and long.[4]

• *A Final Thought*
Read again 13:48-52 and account for the joy of the disciples in view of all that was transpiring at that time.

4. E.M. Bounds, *Purpose in Prayer* (Chicago: Moody, n.d.), p. 40.

Lesson 13

Jerusalem Council

Before Paul could resume his missionary crusade, the problem of Gentile salvation reappeared. This problem had faced the church earlier (chaps. 10-11). On Paul's first mission to the churches of south Galatia, many Gentiles were saved as a result of the apostle's preaching of the gospel of grace. After he left those regions, certain Judaizers from Jerusalem went to the new groups of Christians and told them they needed to observe various rites of Moses' law, such as circumcision, in order to be truly saved. When Paul heard of this subversive work of the Judaizers, he wrote a letter (Galatians) to all the churches, confirming what he had preached to them, that faith in Christ's atoning work was the only condition of salvation. Read Galatians for background to this lesson.

Since the problem of Gentile salvation was more than just a local problem, the church at Antioch, which personally heard a group of Judaizers setting forth their "new" theology, sent a delegation to Jerusalem, including Paul and Barnabas, to discuss the question with the church there. The meeting that took place there has since been called the Jerusalem Council.

• **Paragraph Divisions** At verses 1, 6, 22, 30

• **Observations and Questions**
1. Contrast the opening of the passage (v. 2) with the ending (vv. 31-33).

_____

_____

_____

2. Note the strict legalism of verse 1: "Except ye be circumcised . . . ye cannot be saved." Are there any voices in professing Christendom today similar to this?

_____

_____

3. What did each of these contribute to the council's decision:
Peter (vv. 7-11)

_____

Barnabas and Paul (v. 12)

_____

James (vv. 7-14; 19-21)

_____

Prophets (vv. 15-17)

_____

4. Was the abstinence recommendation (vv. 20, 29) a surrender of the basic principle involved? Justify your answer.

_____

_____

5. What do you learn from this chapter about how the church should face problems and transact business?

_____

_____

6. What good traits of the apostles are manifested in this story?

_____

_____

_____

_____

_____

• *Applications*
1. example to follow:

_____

2. sin to avoid:

_____

3. command to obey:

4. promise to claim:

• *A Topical Study* LAW AND GRACE

> But we believe that though the grace of the Lord Jesus Christ we shall be saved, even as they (15:11).

The entrance of Christ into world history, by way of the incarnation, has been misinterpreted by some as the beginning of a new way of salvation or the revelation of a different kind of God. But the way of salvation has always been the same, offered by the same God to all mankind: by God's grace, through man's faith. Christ's atoning blood covers the sins of all who believe, regardless of when they have lived.

As to principle at work, God's law and God's grace have always been with man. As to events in the two eras of Old and New Testament, the laws are prominent in the Old Testament, and the Son is prominent in the New.

THE LAWS AND THE SON   **Chart K**

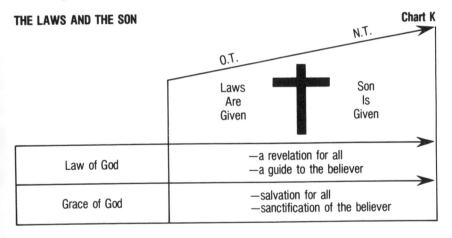

Law and grace are both a vital part of the design of God concerning man's salvation. Each reveals a different aspect of the Person and work of God. In Chart L are listed various comparisons which the Bible makes of law and grace. Read the verses that are cited.

• *A Final Thought*

When the question of the Jerusalem Council was settled, the apostles were not sidetracked to a solely negativistic or defensive ministry. Not long after the recommendation was delivered to the church at Antioch (15:30) Paul and his co-workers were busy again "teaching and preaching the word of the Lord" (15:35).[1]

1. Paul of course delivered the council's recommendation to other churches as well (cf. 16:4), but this was not his main message.

LAW AND GRACE

Chart L

LAW	GRACE
"The law is holy" (Rom. 7:12).	Grace is glorious (Eph. 1:6).
"The law is spiritual" (Rom. 7:14).	The Spirit is of grace (Heb. 10:29).
The principle by which righteousness is demanded from man (Ezek. 18:5-9).	The principle by which righteousness is supplied to man (Rom. 10:4).
A rule of conduct.	Unmerited favor.
Shows us our need.	Shows God's provision to meet that need.
Reveals sin (Rom. 7:7).	Condemns sin (Rom. 8:3).
Reveals the holiness of God (Ex. 20:1-21).	Reveals the love of God (Titus 3:4-5).
God's purity seen in Christ.	God's riches given by Christ.
Appeals to action.	Appeals to faith.
Mount Sinai; the old covenant; bondage (Gal. 4:19-31).	Mount Calvary; the new covenant; freedom (cf. Rom. 6:14).
The standard of God's judgment.	The motive of God's redemption.
Makes nothing perfect (Heb. 7:19; Rom. 3:20).	Imparts to the Christian corresponding graces (Gal. 5:22-23).
Cannot save (Rom. 3:20; 7:7).	Salvation is by grace (Acts 15:11; Eph. 2:8).
Points man to Christ (Gal. 3:24).	Given to man through Christ (Gal. 3:10, 13).

Lesson 14

Second Missionary Journey

Two burdens lay heavy on Paul's heart: needs of Galatian churches and of people in regions beyond. The south Galatian churches needed encouragement and strengthening, and those in the regions beyond needed to hear the gospel. These were the reasons for Paul's second missionary journey.

Study the map on Chart A. Fix in your mind the locations of the major cities of this journey, so that when you read the biblical text you can visualize the movements from place to place. Observe that the ministry of the second journey was concentrated in Macedonia and Greece, rather than in Asia Minor, where one would have expected the next work to be accomplished.

• Paragraph Divisions

You may want to divide this lesson into smaller study units, such as 15:36-16:15; 16:16-40; 17:1-15; 17:16-34; 18:1-22. Paragraph divisions can be determined accordingly.

• Observations and Questions

1. Record below the main events of this journey, by way of acquaintance:

15:36-40   —Start   _____

15:40–16:10 —Derbe to Troas _____

16:11-40   —Philippi   _____

17:1-9   —Thessalonica   _____

17:10-14   —Berea   _____

17:15-34   —Athens   _____

72

18:1-17   —Corinth   _____

18:18-22   —Return   _____

2. Record on Chart M what you learn from this passage about the gospel's message, men and methods.

THE GOSPEL'S MESSAGE, MEN, AND METHODS   **Chart M**

MESSAGE	MEN	METHODS

3. What is taught here about:
prayer

_____

_____

will of God

_____

_____

persecution

_____

_____

• *Applications*

1. example to follow:

_____

2. sin to avoid:

_____

3. command to obey:

_____

4. promise to claim:

_____

5. prayer to echo:

_____

• *A Topical Study* REPENTANCE

> God . . . now commandeth all men every where to repent
> (Acts 17:30*b*).

The verse quoted above shows the universality of the divine command of repentance. Peter wrote that God desires that everyone should come to repentance (2 Pet. 3:9). The heart of Christ's parting message was that "repentance and remission of sins" (Luke 24:47) should be preached to all nations. Repentance applies universally because sin, which is its subject, is universal.

Unfortunately, the message of repentance is shunned or despised by many people today. Herbert Lockyer writes:

> It is contended that our forefathers placed too much emphasis on poignancy of grief as a necessary element in true repentance, in so far as they permitted any idea of merit to attach to the experience. Yet surely they were right in insisting on a deep and genuine upturning of the soul. In our age we have swung to the other direction. We seldom hear the old prophetic cry, "Break up your fallow ground, sow not among thorns" (Jeremiah 4:3). This generation, with all its religion, has lost the sense of sin. . . . The plow of conviction is never driven deep into the human soil.[1]

Let us look to the Bible for some answers to questions concerning this important doctrine of repentance. Read in your Bible all the references cited below.

1. Herbert Lockyer, *All the Doctrines of the Bible* (Grand Rapids: Zondervan, 1964), p. 169.

I. JUST WHAT IS REPENTANCE?

Repentance is basically a change of direction, a complete turnabout. Most of the words translated "repent" in the Bible have this underlying idea. Repentance for sin is such a sorrow for sin, or abhorrence of sin, such a change of mind about it, as leads the sinner to turn away from it with all his heart and identify himself with the gracious God who thus is stirring his heart to draw him to Himself.

Repentance leads to forgiveness of sins (Luke 24:47) and so, mixed with faith (Acts 20:21; Mark 1:15), brings salvation. Like faith, repentance is a gift of a gracious God (Acts 5:31; 11:18; 2 Tim. 2:25; Rom. 2:4; Jonah 4:2). Repentance is not mere tears or solemn resolutions. It is genuine transformation of a person's whole being, involving intellect, emotions, and will. These are discussed below.

II. WHO SHOULD REPENT?

Everyone, saved and unsaved, should repent, because everyone sins. Read Acts 5:31; 17:29-30; Matthew 9:13; Revelation 2:4-5.

III. HOW IS REPENTANCE EXPERIENCED?

There is no one standard experience of repentance, as to time, intensity, awareness of all that is involved, and such other aspects. but all true repentance involves a person's *whole* being: his intellect, emotions, and will.

1. Intellect—This is a change of *view*, regarding sin, God, and the person repenting (Ps. 51:3, 7; Job 42:1-6; Luke 15:17-19).

2. Emotions—This is a change of *feeling*, a deep sorrow for sins committed (Ps. 6:6; 51:1-2; Jer. 31:18-19; Joel 2:12; 2 Cor. 7:8-10).

3. Will—This is a change of *will*, the decision that leads to action in accord with the change of view and feeling (Isa. 55:7; Matt. 3:2, 8; Luke 13:3; Acts 2:38-40; 20:21; Rom. 2:4-6; 2 Cor. 7:9-11; 2 Pet. 3:9, 11; Rev. 2:5).

Read Psalm 119:57-60, and observe the psalmist's intellect, emotions, and will in action.

Involved in true repentance are confession of sin (Hosea 14:1-2; Luke 18:13-14), and turning away *from* sin (Ezek. 14:6; Isa. 55:7) *to* the performance of good (1 Thess. 1:9). The son in Matthew 21:28-29 illustrates true repentance.

IV. WHAT ARE THE RESULTS OF REPENTANCE?

Among the many fruits of repentance are pardon for the sinner (Luke 24:47; Acts 3:19); restored fellowship (Ps. 51:11-12); service and abundant living (Ps. 51:12-15); and even joy in heaven (Luke 15:7-10).

V. DOES GOD REPENT?

Verses like Genesis 6:6-7, Exodus 32:14, and 2 Samuel 24:16 speak of God's repenting. This cannot mean that God changes with respect to Himself, for He is the unchanging One: "I am the Lord, I change not" (Mal. 3:6). When God repents it is only with respect to certain changes in His creatures.

> God's immutability is not like that of the stone that does not respond to changes about it, but like that of the column of mercury which rises and falls according as the temperature changes. His immutability consists in His always doing the right and in adapting the treatment of His creatures to the variations in their character and conduct.[2]

(Read Jer. 18:8; 26:12-13; Joel 2:13; Ex. 32:9-14; Jonah 3:10.)

For a concluding study on repentance, read the following passage which record times when repentance was preached:

1. by the prophets (Deut. 30:10; 2 Kings 17:13; Jer. 8:6; Ezek. 14:6; 18:30)
2. by John the Baptist (Matt. 3:2; Mark 1:15)
3. by Christ (Matt. 4:17; Luke 13:3, 5)
4. by apostles (Mark 6:12; Acts 2:38; 3:19; 20:21; 26:20)

• A Final Thought

The most sobering fact we could ever declare to this Christ-rejecting world is what Paul concluded his Mars hill message with, that God "has fixed a day, when He is to judge the world righteously through a Man destined for the task" (Acts 17:31*a*, Berkeley).

No wonder God commands "all men everywhere to repent" (17:30).

---

2. Henry C. Thiessen, *Introductory Lectures in Systematic Theology* (Grand Rapids: Eerdmans, 1956), p. 128.

Third Missionary Journey

The basic purposes of Paul's third missionary journey were the same as those of the second. They were to spread the gospel to unevangelized cities and to strengthen the young converts in places already visited.

The geographical coverage of each of the three journeys, with respect to unevangelized territories, is shown in Chart N.

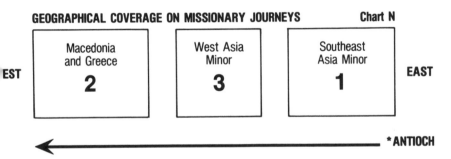

GEOGRAPHICAL COVERAGE ON MISSIONARY JOURNEYS   **Chart N**

EST	Macedonia and Greece **2**	West Asia Minor **3**	Southeast Asia Minor **1**	EAST

← _____ * ANTIOCH

Observe that Paul bypassed western Asia Minor on his second journey, doing most of his work in Macedonia and Greece. This was by direction of the Holy Spirit (recall the Macedonian vision recorded in 16:6-12). So it was natural for his third tour that he should be led to spend most of his time (three years) in western Asia Minor (with Ephesus at the hub).

• Observations and Questions

1. As you read the passage of this lesson the first time, refer to a map in order to visualize the geography of the journey.
2. Record the main events and ministries of Paul in these segments:

Follow-up: Galatia and Phrygia (18:23)

_____

_____

New: Ephesus and vicinity (18:24-19:41)

_____

_____

_____

_____

Follow-up: Macedonia and Greece (20:1-6)

_____

_____

Concluding: Troas to Jerusalem (20:7–21:17)

_____

_____

3. Note references in the text to duration of ministries for this journey. The whole journey extended from A.D. 52 to 56.
4. What is recorded for this journey concerning the following:
a. Paul's message

_____

_____

b. opposition to Paul

_____

_____

c. miracles

_____

_____

d. fruit of the Word

_____

_____

• *Applications*
1. example to follow:

_____

_____

2. sin to avoid:

_____

3. command to obey:

_____

4. promise to claim:

_____

• *A Topical Study* IDOLATRY

> The city of the Ephesians is a worshipper of the great goddess Diana (Acts 19:35).

I. DESCRIPTION

Idolatry is attachment and devotion to anything that dethrones God from the heart. For example, covetousness is idolatry (Eph. 5:5; Col. 3:5). The person or thing that one most honors, upon which one most strongly sets his affection, to which one gives first place in his life, is the person or thing that individual worships. If that person is not God, such worship is idolatry.

The Lord alone is the One to whom worship belongs (Matt. 4:10; Rev. 19:10; 22:8-9). The Lord God alone is entitled to the highest honor, the strongest affection, the first place in the thought and life of man. And when man puts anything else in this place that belongs to God, he is guilty of idolatry.

The Athenians, as seen in Acts 19, gave first place to Diana, their idol. Many people today make money their idol, giving it first place in their thought and life. Others make pleasure, self-gratification, or self-will the idol that they worship. Unless God has first place in our hearts and lives, we are guilty of idolatry. Ponder this much.

II. WARNINGS

Israel, throughout her history, was warned against idolatry (see Deut. 6:12-15). It was idolatry, stubbornly persisted in, that brought on the judgment of the captivities (2 Chron. 36:14-17; cf. Jer. 25:2-11).

Christians are warned against idolatry (1 Cor. 10:6-7, 14-15; 2 Cor. 6:16-18; 1 John 5:21). This warning is sorely needed in these days when the idols of the world are proving so attractive to the professed followers of Christ.

III. CONSEQUENCES

The consequences of idolatry are fatal:

1. No idolater has any inheritance in the kingdom of God (Eph. 5:5).

2. The wrath of God comes upon idolaters (Eph. 5:5-6; Col. 3:5-6).

3. Idolaters are to be cast into the lake of fire (Rev. 21:7-8).

• *A Topical Study* THE SCRIPTURES

> I commend you to . . . the word of his grace, which is able to build you up (Acts 20:32).

When Paul spoke the above words to the Ephesian elders, all of the Bible had not yet been written. Yet the Bible was considered to be indispensable for leading souls to God and building them up in the faith.

The importance of Bible study cannot be overestimated. Knowledge of the Bible is a supreme need in the church today. Ignorance of the Bible on the part of multitudes of Christians is alarming. Someone has said that all the sin, error, heresy, and worldliness that has ever been in the church has come through the neglect of God's Word—neglect to know it and obey it.

The Scriptures played an important part in the lives of God's servants in Bible times. Read the following passages with reference to the men cited:

Moses (Deut. 6:6-9; 17:18-20)

Joshua (Joshua 1:7-8)

David (Pss. 1:1-2; 119:97)

Josiah (2 Kings 23:1-2)

Ezra (Neh. 8:1-8; 9:3)

Paul (Acts 20:32)

For further study, read these passages which describe some of the fruits of the Bible study:

1. knowledge of sin (2 Kings 22:8, 11-13; Heb. 4:12; Rom. 3:20)

2. repentance (2 Kings 22:11-13, 19)

3. revival and reformation (2 Kings 23:1-3)

4. saving faith in Christ (Acts 17:11-12)

5. prosperity (Joshua 1:8; Ps. 1:2-3)

6. burning hearts (Luke 24:27, 32)

> Neither count I my life dear unto myself, so that I might finish my course with joy (Acts 20:24).

Paul did not fear death; indeed, he seemed to look forward to it with longing (see Phil. 1:23-24; 2 Tim. 4:6-8). One reason for this was that he understood so clearly what is the destiny of believers. Paul had lived so in the will of God that he knew, according to God's promises, he had a right to claim many of the rewards of faithfulness. He seemed to long to enter into the enjoyment of his possessions.

I. TO BELIEVERS THERE IS REALLY NO DEATH

Read John 8:51; 11:26; 1 John 2:17. For believers, to die is to be with Christ. The body is placed in the grave to await resurrection day (the rapture), but the spirit is taken to Christ (cf. Acts 7:60 with 1 Thess. 4:13-15).

II. WHERE BELIEVERS SHALL BE

Believers shall live throughout eternity with the Lord (John 14:3; 1 Thess. 4:17), in a place which Christ has prepared (John 14:2), a place of beauty and purity and joy (Rev. 22:1-5; 21:4). One writer says, "Here a few drops of joy enter into us; there we enter into joy as vessels put into a sea of happiness."

III. WHAT BELIEVERS SHALL BE LIKE

Believers shall be like Christ (1 John 3:2). From the time of the rapture they shall have a glorious resurrection body like His (Phil. 3:20-21).

IV. THE REWARDS OF BELIEVERS

Rewards will vary according to fidelity in service. We are *saved* by faith but *rewarded* according to our own works (cf. Matt. 6:20; 1 Cor. 3:11-15).

1. Believers who endure temptation shall receive a crown of life (James 1:12; cf. Rev. 2:10).
2. Believers who have loved His appearing will receive a crown of righteousness (2 Tim. 4:8).

3. Believers who have been faithful undershepherds will receive a crown of glory (1 Pet. 5:1-4).

4. Believers who have part in the first resurrection (the resurrection referred to in 1 Thess. 4:16-17) shall reign with Christ a thousand years (Rev. 20:5-6).

5. Believers who are "overcomers" shall receive the rewards promised (Rev. 2:7, 11, 17, 26-27; 3:4-5, 12, 21).

6. Fellowship with God for eternity will be the greatest reward of the believer (read 1 Cor. 9:25; 1 Thess. 2:19; Luke 19:11-28; 2 Tim. 2:11-12).

• *A Final Thought*

Paul's farewell message to the Ephesian elders (Acts 20:17-35) deserves careful analysis. As a final exercise for this lesson, list the many desirable traits of Christian service shown in the message, whether they are exemplified by Paul or appealed to in his charge to the elders.

Lesson 16
Acts 21:18–22:29

Paul Before the Mob

Paul the missionary became Paul the prisoner and remained in bonds for the rest of the story of Acts. But chains and prison walls did not keep this man of God from bearing a clear witness of the gospel by speech and by letter. His testimony, courage, faith, wisdom, patience, and concern for others are some of the wonderful traits that are manifested in these closing chapters of Acts. As a preview of the main movements of the remainder of Acts, study Chart O.

APPEARANCES OF PAUL THE PRISONER
21:18—28:31   **Chart O**

21:18	22:30	23:31		25:13	27:1 28:31
Before the Mob	Before the Council	Before the Governors Felix Festus		Before a King Agrippa	Awaiting Trial Before the Emperor (Caesar)
At Jerusalem		At Caesarea			To Rome
A.D. 56					A.D. 61

Paul's verbal defenses played an important part in this five-year period of incarceration for the apostle. You may want to read one time all the defenses he made, for comparative purposes: 22:1-21; 23:1, 3, 6; 24:10b-21; 25:8, 10-11; 26:2-23, 25-27, 29; 28:17-20, 23-31.

The story of this lesson is the story of divine protection for a servant of God in the hands of a violent, murderous mob.

• *Paragraph Divisions* At verses 21:18, 27, 37, 40b; 22:6, 12, 17, 22

83

• Observations and Questions

1. Read the passage in four parts, according to the following breakdown. Record the main content of each part:

21:18-26

_____

21:27-36

_____

21:37-22:21

_____

22:22-29

_____

2. Identify the false accusations of the people in 21:18-36. What different actions were taken to correct the false charges (vv. 20-26 and 37-40*a*)?

_____

_____

3. Study carefully Paul's personal testimony of 22:1-21. What was his view of himself before and after conversion?

_____

Observe the preeminence he gave to God and Christ in the testimony.

4. What was the word that closed the ears of Paul's audience (22:22)?

_____

5. On what basis was Paul spared scourging (22:25-29)?

_____

Consult a Bible dictionary or encyclopedia for a description of this tormenting procedure of forcing submission and confession from the victims (read Acts 16:22; 2 Cor. 11:25; Matt. 27:26).

• Applications

1. example to follow:

_____

2. sin to avoid:

_____

3. command to obey:

_____

4. promise to claim:

_____

5. prayer to echo:

_____

● *A Topical Study* THE BELIEVER'S IDENTIFICATION WITH CHRIST

> And I persecuted . . . men and women (22:4).
> I am Jesus of Nazareth, whom thou persecutest (22:8).

In 22:7-8 Jesus accuses Saul of persecuting Him. Yet we know from Acts 9:1-2 and elsewhere that it was the disciples of Jesus whom Saul was persecuting. The explanation is this: Just as God in the Old Testament identified Himself with His people so closely that He considered them one with Himself, and any slight or insult given them as given to Himself (Isa. 63:9; Zech. 2:7-8), so Christ identifies Himself with believers so closely that they are reckoned one with Himself (Matt. 10:40; Acts 9:1, 4-5).

The believer is identified with Christ in at least these seven particulars:

1. *In the new nature.* We are born with human nature which is utterly corrupt and incapable of pleasing God (Eph. 2:3; Rom. 8:7-8). When we believe on Christ He imparts to us a new nature, His own divine nature. That is why, on becoming Christians, we begin to despise the things that we once loved (e.g., envy, uncleanness, worldliness) and begin to love the things that we once shunned (e.g., righteousness, holiness, prayer). It is true that the old nature remains with us after we are saved, bringing about a conflict between the old and the new. But the new nature is the ruling nature and, since it is of Christ, we are intimately identified with Him.

2. *In the new life* (Col. 3:4; 1 John 5:12). Christ is life (John 14:6), and when we have Him dwelling within us by His Holy Spirit, we are one with Him in life, related to Him as the branch is to the vine (John 15:5). From the moment of the new birth we have not only physical life but spiritual life, the life of Christ.

3. *In relationships* (John 20:17; Heb. 2:11; Rom. 8:16). Being one with Christ in nature and life, we are necessarily one with

Him in His relationships. His Father is our Father. God looks upon the believer as one with His Son and therefore loves the believer as He loves His Son. The believer is just as near and just as dear to God as Jesus Christ is.

> Near, so very near to God, nearer I cannot be,
> For in the person of His Son, I'm just as near as He.
> Dear, so very dear to God, dearer I cannot be,
> For in the person of His Son, I'm just as dear as He.

4. *In service* (John 17:18; Matt. 28:20). As believers, our work in the world is the continuation of the work that Christ began.

5. *In suffering* (Phil. 1:29; 3:10; Col. 1:24). Being one with Christ in nature, life, relationships and service, we must expect to suffer with Him. The things that pain Him will pain us; those who hate Him will hate us. The servant is not above his Master. "Yea, and all that will live godly in Christ Jesus shall suffer persecution" (2 Tim. 3:12). If we are not suffering in any way for Christ, is it because we are not living godly in Him?

6. *In inheritance* (Rom. 8:16-17). Meditate on all that belongs to God in the universe. God's only begotten Son is heir to all His Father's possessions, and we, being one with Christ, are joint heirs with Him.

7. *In future glory in the Kingdom* (Rom. 8:18-21; 1 Pet. 2:9; Rev. 1:6; 5:10; 2 Tim. 2:12). Think of being associated and identified with Christ in His glorious reign.

Our identification with Christ is not without responsibility. We are accepted of God in His Son—should we not be burdened for those in the world who are not of His fold? The day of the Lord approaches quickly, when the earth and its works shall be burned up (2 Pet. 3:10)—should not our behavior now be consecrated and pleasing to God? (Read 2 Pet. 3:11).

• *A Final Thought*
All Christian service should be for the glory of the Lord, not for the praise of man. Paul was a successful missionary, and he rightly directed all glory to God. After he had saluted the elders at Jerusalem, "he declared particularly *what things God had wrought* among the Gentiles by his ministry. And when they heard it, *they glorified the Lord*" (Acts 21:19-20, italics added).

Paul Before the Council

Paul was delivered from the mob's frenzy, but his trials continued. Next he went before the Sanhedrin. This was the highest Jewish tribunal of his day (called "council" in most of our Bibles). This is the story of the present lesson.

The Sanhedrin was composed of seventy members, plus the president, who was the high priest. Its members were scribes (interpreters of the Law), elders (older men serving as local counselors and judges) and chief priests (various members of high priestly families). The Sanhedrin's jurisdiction was mainly over religious and civil matters, occasionally over criminal cases.

There were two religious factions represented in the membership of the Sanhedrin: Pharisees and Sadducees. The Pharisees, which were the most influential, held to a large body of traditions in addition to the written law. The Sadducees accepted only the latter. The passage of this lesson indicates that the Pharisees believed in the resurrection of the dead and in spirits, whereas the Sadducees denied both (23:8).

For more information about the Sanhedrin, Pharisees, Sadducees, scribes, and elders, refer to a Bible dictionary or encyclopedia.

● *Paragraph Divisions* At verses 22:30; 23:1, 6, 11, 12, 16, 23, 26

● *Observations and Questions*
1. Claudius Lysias was the name of the chief captain who rescued Paul from the fanatical mob (cf. 23:26). What was his view regarding the people's charges against Paul (see 22:30; 23:28-29)?

_____

_____

2. Observe the following qualities of Paul:
a. honesty (cf. 23:1)
b. boldness (23:3)
c. respect (23:5)
d. wisdom (23:6, 17)
3. Read Exodus 22:28 in connection with Acts 23:5.
4. Does 23:11 imply that Paul may have begun to become discouraged and pessimistic?

_____

5. What does 23:11 reveal concerning whether or not it was God's will that Paul should have come to Jerusalem at this time?

_____

_____

6. Note the reference to Paul's sister's son in 23:16. This is one of the few references in the New Testament to Paul's family.
7. What were God's methods of protecting Paul in these experiences?

_____

_____

_____

• *Applications*
1. example to follow:

_____

2. sin to avoid:

_____

3. command to obey:

_____

4. promise to claim:

_____

• *A Topical Study* RESURRECTION

> Of the hope and resurrection of the dead I am called in question (23:6).

It is plain from the gospels and epistles that the subject of the resurrection of the dead occupied a large place in the witnessing and preaching of the apostles. Read these passages: Acts 1:21-22; 2:24, 29-32; 4:2, 33; 17:18; 23:6; 24:15, 21; 1 Corinthians 15:12-23.

I. THE RESURRECTION OF JESUS CHRIST

The resurrection of the body of Jesus Christ is one of the two fundamental truths of the gospel (1 Cor. 15:1-4). "It is the Gibraltar of Christian evidences, the Waterloo of infidelity and rationalism."[1] The crucifixion loses its meaning without the resurrection. Without the resurrection, the death of Christ was only the heroic death of a noble martyr; with the resurrection it is the atoning death of the Son of God. Disprove the resurrection of Jesus Christ, and Christian faith is in vain (1 Cor. 15:14, 17). But Jesus Christ did rise from the grave. Christian *faith* rests upon a solid and unassailable foundation of *fact*.

II. THE FACT OF JESUS' RESURRECTION

The main evidences of the fact of the resurrection of Jesus' body are:

1. Testimony of people who saw the empty tomb (e.g., John 29:8; 13-16; Luke 24:10)

2. Testimony of people who saw the resurrected Christ (e.g., Luke 24:33-34; John 21; Acts 10:40-41; 1 Cor. 15:5-8)

3. Testimony of history, as to the miraculous rise, power and endurance of the church.

4. Testimony of prophecy before the event (e.g., Old Testament: Ps. 2:7, cf. Acts 13:31-37; Ps. 16:10-11; Christ: Matt. 16:21; 17:9-23; Mark 8:31)

5. Testimony of Christ Himself, after He was resurrected (Luke 24:39-48)

III. THE SIGNIFICANCES OF JESUS' RESURRECTION

The resurrection of Christ is not only a *fact*—it is also a mighty *factor*. It is not only a *doctrine*—it is also a *dynamic*.[2] These are its major significances:

1. It confirms the deity of Christ (Rom. 1:4).

2. It guarantees the Father's acceptance of the work of Christ (Phil. 2:9).

1. R.A. Torrey, *What the Bible Teaches* (Westwood, N.J.: Revell, 1898), p. 166.
2. Herbert Lockyer, *All the Doctrines of the Bible* (Grand Rapids: Zondervan, 1964), p. 53.

3. It makes possible our justification, regeneration, and sanctification (Rom. 4:25; 5-10; 6:4-5, 9; 8:34; 1 Cor. 6:14; 15:17, 20-22; Eph. 1:20; Phil. 3:10; 1 Pet. 1:3).

4. It makes certain a final judgment (Acts 17:31).

5. It assures the resurrection of the bodies of saints (1 Cor. 15:20).

IV. THE TWO RESURRECTIONS

Miracles of the dead restored to life are recorded in the Old Testament, the gospels (e.g., Matt. 27:52-53) and Acts. But these were not of the same sort as Christ's resurrection, for the people involved returned eventually to the grave.

The Bible speaks of two resurrections other than Christ's (John 5:29; Acts 24:15). The one is resurrection unto life (1 Cor. 15:22-23; 1 Thess. 4:14-17; Rev. 20:5). The other is resurrection unto judgment (John 5:28-29; Rev. 20:11-15). Only the bodies of believers are involved in the resurrection unto life, which will take place at the second coming of Christ. The bodies of unbelievers are involved in the second resurrection, which brings on the great white throne judgment (Rev. 20:11-15). The destiny of all unbelievers after this life is a tragic one indeed.

• *A Final Thought*

Roman citizenship could be bought (Acts 22:28), inherited ("free born," 22:28), or won. Paul was born a Roman citizen, for his parents were Roman citizens. Citizenship in heaven is not by human heritage, and can neither be bought or won. One needs to be born again of the Father through faith in His Son.

Lesson 18

Acts 23:31–25:12

Paul Before the Governors

Felix and Festus were the Judean governors to whom Paul was next brought for trial and disposition. This was concerning the Jerusalem Jews' false charges. Two things stand out in the story of this lesson: (1) the blunt falsehood of the charges by Paul's accusers, and (2) the slow deliberations of suave and selfish politicians.

Felix was governor of Judea, residing at the capital city, Caesarea, from A.D. 52-57. About two years after Paul's first appearance before him he was recalled to Rome and replaced by Porcius Festus. Festus ruled from A.D. 59 to 61.

• **Paragraph Divisions** At verses 23:31; 24:1, 10, 22, 24; 25:1, 6

• **Observations and Questions**
1. Compare Tertullus's and Paul's personal salutations to Felix (24:2-4 and 24:10-11*a*).

_____

_____

2. List the individual charges cited by Tertullus (24:5-9) on Chart P. Which ones are answered by Paul, and how (vv. 11-21)? List these also on the chart.
3. What did Paul testify regarding his
worship:

_____

hope:

_____

behavior:

_____

91

4. What were Felix's two special interests in Paul (24:24-26)?

_____

_____

CHARGES AND REPLIES Chart P

Tertullus's Charges	Paul's Replies

Account for his trembling (24:25).

5. Compare Felix and Festus as people-pleasers (24:27 and 25:9).

_____

6. Why did Paul request trial at Rome (25:11) rather than at Jerusa-lem (25:9-10)?

_____

• *Applications*
1. example to follow:

_____

2. sin to avoid:

_____

3. command to obey:

_____

4. promise to claim:

_____

• *A Topical Study* JUDGMENT

> And as he reasoned of righteousness, temperance, and judgment to come, Felix trembled (24:25).

All thoughts of final judgment are sobering thoughts, in view of who the Judge is. The Bible speaks of various judgments such as those of angels and the world (1 Cor. 6:2-3), Jews (Rev. 12:6, 13-17), and nations (Matt. 25:32). The two most important judgments are those of the unbelievers and of the believers.

I. JUDGMENT OF UNBELIEVERS

This is the great white throne judgment, the last and most awful of God's judgments (read Rev. 20:11-15; Matt. 10:15; Acts 2:20; 2 Pet. 2:3-4, 7; Jude 6). God will judge all lost souls by His Son Jesus (John 5:23; Acts 17:31). Unbelievers will stand before God without their names written in the Lamb's book of Life, and they will be cast into the lake of fire for eternity (Rev. 3:5; 20:12-15; Luke 10:20), where Satan and his hosts will also be cast.

II. JUDGMENT OF BELIEVERS

The sins of believers have already been judged at the cross, in the person of Jesus Christ. He bore all our sins, dying for them, paying the full penalty. Death for Christ meant justification for the believer (read John 5:24; Rom. 5:9; 8:1; 2 Cor. 5:21; Heb. 9:26-28; 10:10, 14-18; 1 Pet. 2:24; 3:18).

The deeds and works of heaven await a future day of judgment. All believers will appear before the Bema ("judgment") seat of Christ, to be judged for the works done in the body. They must give account of how they used the talents (Matt. 25:14-30), pounds (Luke 19:11-27), and opportunities (Matt. 20:1-6) that had been entrusted to them. Every work must come into judgment (Rom. 14:10; 1 Cor. 3:11-15; 4:5; 2 Cor. 5:10; Gal. 6:7; Eph. 6:8; Col. 3:24-25). The consequence of each work is either reward or loss of reward. Fire of this judgment will consume works of wood, hay, or stubble; works likened to gold, silver, and precious stones will remain forever (1 Cor. 3:11-15).

The judgment seat of Christ will take place at His second coming (Matt. 16:27; Luke 14:14; 1 Cor. 4:5; 2 Tim. 4:8; Rev. 22:12).

III. COMPARISONS OF THE TWO ETERNAL STATES

The Bible teaches that there is a great gulf, literally and figuratively, between the future destiny of believers and that of unbelievers.

1. Believers have life (not merely existence but perfect life) eternally (John 11:25-26; 17:3; 1 John 2:17). Unbelievers have death (nonexistence but separation from God) eternally (1 Tim. 5:6; John 3:36; Rev. 21:8; cf. 20:10).

2. Believers will be forever with Christ (John 14:3; 1 Thess. 4:17). Unbelievers will be forever separated from Christ (2 Thess. 1:8-9).

3. The love of God abides upon the believer (2 Cor. 13:14). The wrath of God abides upon the unbeliever (John 3:36).

4. Believers will have eternal joy (John 15:11; Rev. 21:4). Unbelievers will have eternal torment (Rev. 14:9-11; 20:15).

5. Believers will be in heaven (John 14:2-3; 1 Pet. 1:3-5). Unbelievers will be in hell (Rev. 20:14-15).

• *A Final Thought*
As Christians we are to look to the future, in "hope toward God" (Acts 24:15); and we are to walk acceptably in the present, with "conscience void of offense toward God" (24:16). This is another way of saying that God should be the center of our lives. Is He this in all things?

Lesson 19
Acts 25:13–26:32

Paul Before a King

Paul appealed to Caesar, giving Festus a new problem of how to charge him before the emperor. Festus mentioned this to Agrippa[1] when this king was visiting Festus with his sister Bernice on the occasion of the official welcome of Festus as new governor of Judea. Agrippa, who was an "expert" in Jewish customs and problems (Acts 26:3), became very interested in the case and asked for the opportunity to hear Paul's testimony himself. What Paul said, and the reactions of both Festus and Agrippa, constitute the story of this lesson.

- **Paragraph Divisions** At verses 25:13, 23; 26:1, 4, 12, 19, 24, 30

- **Observations and Questions**
1. Observe the following outline as you read the passage the first time:
Festus briefs Agrippa (25:13-22).
Paul presented to Agrippa (25:23-27).
Paul's testimony and defense (26:1-23).
Response of Festus and Agrippa (26:24-29).
Rulers' conclusions (26:30-32).
2. Does it appear from 25:19 that Festus was familiar with the gospel message about Jesus?

---

1. This King Agrippa was Herod Agrippa II, son of Agrippa I, the Herod of 12:1. Agrippa II would have succeeded his father to the throne of Judea at his father's death in A.D. 44, had he not been so young (seventeen). Instead he was given a small kingdom in Lebanon, which he later relinquished in exchange for a larger domain located in southern Syria.

Compare also his reaction of 26:24. Is the same kind of reaction voiced by unbelievers today against true witnesses of the gospel?

_____

3. What commendable trait of Festus appears in 25:23-27?

_____

4. Paul's defense contains the third Acts account of his conversion. Compare all three: 9:1-9 (the event); 22:1-11 (Paul's testimony before the people); 26:4-18 (Paul's testimony before the rulers). What is new in this third passage?

_____

What things are prominent in Paul's recollection of his conversion experience?

_____

_____

5. If salvation is attained by being religious, Paul would have been a saved man before he ever started on his way to Damascus. Explain this on the basis of 26:4-7.

_____

6. What was Paul's appeal in 26:8?

_____

7. What are the contrasting words in 26:18?

_____

What does this verse teach about the way of salvation?

_____

8. What does the paragraph 26:19-23 teach about obedience and trust?

_____

_____

9. Observe how clear it was to Paul that writers of the Old Testament (Moses and the prophets) prophesied of the Messiah's death

96

and resurrection. (The title "Christ" was the Greek equivalent of the Hebrew title "Messiah.")

10. Analyze carefully the dialogue between Paul and Agrippa. Compare the readings of verse 28 in various versions. The literal rendering is, "In a little, you are persuading me to make a Christian." If we knew Agrippa's motive behind the words, we would know the meaning of the words. Two possibilities are that they were:

Spoken in sarcasm: "In a short time you think to make me a Christian" (*Revised Standard Version*).

Spoken seriously: "You are with a little effort convincing enough to make me a Christian" (Berkeley).

What do you think was the intent of Agrippa's words?

_____

_____

How important is it to respond to whatever light is given by God?

_____

_____

Is it true that God gives additional light to those who respond to light already given (cf. Matt. 13:12)?

_____

_____

• *Applications*

1. example to follow:

_____

2. sin to avoid:

_____

3. command to obey:

_____

4. promise to claim:

_____

• *A Topical Study* SIN

> To open their eyes, and to turn them from darkness to light, and from the power of Satan unto God, that they may receive forgiveness of sins, and inheritance (Acts 26:18).

This verse tells us that Paul was commissioned to preach to the Gentiles that they might receive forgiveness of sins (negative aspect of salvation) and inheritance (positive aspect). The inheritance does not come without the forgiveness of sins.

The subject of sin is an important subject, for a correct view of salvation depends on a correct view of sin. The following outline shows some of the major aspects of this subject (read all verses cited):

I. DEFINITION OF SIN

Sin is transgression of God's law (1 John 3:4). This law of God is the sovereign, external standard of right and wrong that He has given the human race for its survival and well-being. It is an expression of His nature, and thus it is holy, for He is holy. Sin is missing the mark, deviating from the way of God's will for His creature. Sin is committed in the heart's thoughts and in outward acts (read also Gal. 3:10, 12; James 2:8-12; Rom. 7:7-13). One of Christendom's standard definitions of sin reads: "Sin is any want of conformity unto, or transgression of, any law of God given as a rule to the reasonable creature."

There is the sin of commission (doing what God has told us not to do), and there is the sin of omission (failing to do what God has told us to do). The Ten Commandments are composed of "thou shalts" as well as "thou shalt nots." All sin, of whatever sort and intensity, is an offense against God. And to transgress one law of God is to be guilty of transgressing the whole law of God (James 2:10; read Matt. 5:44; 22:37-39; 28:19; John 13:34; Eph. 4:29; 5:18).

II. ORIGIN OF SIN

Satan is the father of all untruth (John 8:44). His rebellion against his Creator was the first instance of pride and disobedience (read Isa. 14:12-14).

Sin entered the human race through Adam. When Adam, as federal head of the race, sinned, all sinned. This is the principle of representation (Rom. 5:12-21; 1 Cor. 15:22). The same principle of representation works in the hopeful counterpart of Christ's substitutionary death—One dying for all, so that anyone who believes may live.

III. UNIVERSALITY OF SIN

There can be no denying the *fact* of sin: history, conscience, and the Bible are the three strongest witnesses to its reality. That *all* are sinners is clearly taught (see Eccles. 7:20; Isa. 53:6*a*; Rom. 3:10, 12, 19, 23; 1 John 1:8).

IV. CONSEQUENCES OF SIN

The consequences of sin are threefold: depravity, guilt, and penalty.
1. Depravity (degradation, see Rom. 7:18; 8:7; Eph. 4:18; 2 Tim. 3:4).
2. Guilt (condemnation see Rom. 3:19).
3. Penalty (death). The death penalty is basically that of separation and is of two parts. There is physical death (separation of the spirit from the body, cf. Gen. 2:17; 3:19); and there is spiritual death (separation of the spirit from God, Eph. 2:1; Rom. 5:21; 6:23; Ezek. 18:4).

V. DELIVERANCE FROM THE PENALTY OF SIN

There is only one hope of a man for deliverance from the penalty of sin, which is death. That is for one to die in his place, whose death would be accepted as a perfect sacrifice for his sins. Christ is the only One who had died thus, for the sins of the whole world (Heb. 9:26; Acts 4:12). He is saved who accepts this sacrificial gift by faith.

• *A Final Thought*
Satan is not only a real person, he is a powerful foe. But the gospel can transform "from darkness to light, and from the power of Satan unto God" (26:18). We who know the Lord Jesus should be experiencing the blessedness and power of this transformation.

Lesson 20

Voyage to Rome

The perils of Paul's voyage to Rome were not new experiences for this valiant gospel servant. Read 2 Corinthians 11:23-29 to learn what Paul had written a few years earlier on his third missionary journey concerning the many different kinds of perils and hardships that had been his lot since he had become a Christian.

When Paul began the voyage from Caesarea, he was one of many prisoners. By the time the voyage was over, Paul was the hero and virtual leader of the crew and passengers. They key to the change was his *faith in action*. Earlier, the Lord has said to him, "As thou hast testified of me in Jerusalem, so must thou bear witness also at Rome" (Acts 23:11*b*). This assurance of safe arrival, confirmed by a similar word from God in the middle of the storm (27:24), was enough for Paul. In the darkness of the night he saw the stars, and he convinced the ship's crew to work and endure until the storm had subsided. The solid simplicity of the apostle's faith, and the natural way in which he put it into action, are some of the highlights of this fascinating sea adventure.

- **Paragraph Divisions** At verses 27:1, 9, 13, 21, 27, 33, 39; 28:1, 7, 11

- **Observations and Questions**
1. In your first reading of this passage, follow the voyage on a map so that you can visualize the itinerary. Mark the route on the map on Chart A.
2. Notice references to Luke ("we" of 27:1), Julius (27:1), and Aristarchus (27:2).
3. Compare the treatment of Paul at the beginning of the voyage (27:3) and the end (28:16).

4. Read the passage again paragraph by paragraph. Record the highlights of each portion on Chart Q. Note this outline: Promise —Protection—Provision—Performance. Apply this to the life of the believer today.

ACTS 17:1—28:16   **Chart Q**

27:1-8
 	
  9-12
 	
  13-20

27:21-26   Promise
27:27-32
27:33-44   Protection
28:1-10   Provision
28:11-16   Performance

5. You may want to take the allowable liberty of viewing this real voyage of Paul as illustrative of one's journey of life. Record the many illustrations which may be derived from this narrative.

● *Applications*
1. example to follow:

_____

2. sin to avoid:

_____

3. command to obey:

_____

4. promise to claim:

_____

5. prayer to echo:

_____

- *A Topical Study* THANKSGIVING TO GOD

> And when he had thus spoken, he took bread, and gave thanks to God in presence of them all (27:35*a*).

Thanksgiving and praise occupy a large place in the Bible. David, whose psalms are an inspiration for praise, said, "It is a good thing to give thanks unto the Lord, and to sing praises unto thy name, O most High" (Ps. 92:1). Too little place is given to thanksgiving and praise in the life and prayers of the average Christian. The gracious dealings of the Lord with His people make thanksgiving and praise only proper. We need to learn not only the grace of giving but also the grace of saying thank you. That Jesus waits to hear our thanks is told simply in the story of Jesus' healing of ten lepers: "Weren't all ten men made clean? Where are the other nine? Could they not also come back and give thanks to God? Could only this foreigner come?" (Luke 17:17-18, *Good News for Modern Man*).

I. WHY SHOULD WE GIVE THANKS?

1. We are commanded to give thanks (Col. 3:15, 17; 1 Thess. 5:18; Ps. 100:4).
2. Thanksgiving on the part of His children pleases God greatly (Ps. 69:30-31).
3. We have these examples of true thanksgiving:
a. Christ Himself (Matt. 15:36; 26:27; John 11:41; Matt. 11:25).
b. The early Christians as well as holy men and women of the Old Testament (Acts 2:46-47; Luke 24:52-53; Col. 1:9, 12; 1 Chron. 16:7; Dan. 2:23).

II. FOR WHAT SHOULD WE GIVE THANKS?

The things for which we should give thanks are innumerable. Paul says in Ephesians 5:20 that we should give thanks always for all things. Remembering the assurance given us in Romans 8:28, we should thank God even for the things that appear undesirable.

> There is no greater, nor more simple secret of a life of un-interrupted and ever-increasing joyfulness, then rendering thanks for all things. Our disappointments become "His appointments," our sorrows become joys, and our tears become rainbows.[1]

A few of the things for which we should give thanks are as follows:
1. for Jesus Christ (Luke 2:27-28, 36-38)
2. for forgiveness of sin (Ps. 103:1, 3; Col. 1:12)
3. for victory over sin (1 Cor. 15:57; Rom. 7:24-25)
4. for answered prayer (John 11:41; 2 Cor. 1:3-4)
5. for the conversion of others (Rom. 6:17; 2 Thess. 2:13)
6. for the supply of our physical needs (Acts 27:35)

III. HOW SHOULD WE GIVE THANKS TO GOD?

1. Through Christ (Rom. 1:8; Eph. 5:18-20).
2. Definitely, naming definite blessing received (1 Kings 8:15, 20; John 11:41).
3. Always. That is, our attitude of thanksgiving should be continuous.

> Thanksgiving and prayer should be the atmosphere in which we live, the air we breathe, and just as a man keeps right on breathing while doing a thousand other things without even stopping to think how he does it, so we can keep on praising and thanking, and praying while doing a thousand other things.[2]

• A Final Thought
For Paul, the way to Rome was through a storm, but he did not question God's will concerning the way or the course. Destination was his concern, and destination should be our concern as well. What are our goals and purposes in life? Are they God's goals? And are we willing to tread a rough path, if need be, to reach them?

1. R.A. Torrey, *What the Bible Teaches* (Westwood, N.J.: Revell, 1898), p. 465.
2. Ibid., p. 467.

Lesson 21

Acts 28:17-31

Paul's Witness at Rome

The last word of Acts in the original text is *akolutos*, which is translated 'unhindered.' It must have thrilled the heart of Luke as he penned this last word on the scroll, ending his book on such a triumphant note. Preaching and teaching without hindrance! This did not mean without hardship, because Paul, though treated with special favor, was still a prisoner under guard. But in such a situation, there was an open door of opportunity, and Paul was granted the privilege of his long-cherished dream: preaching the gospel in Rome.

As you study this final passage of Acts, try to visualize the setting, and imagine the thoughts going through Paul's mind. Also, read Ephesians, Philippians, Colossians, and Philemon, which were written during this prison stay of Paul, to grasp something of the deep spiritual experience which was his at the time.

• **Paragraph Divisions** At verses 17, 23, 25, 30

• **Observations and Questions**
1. Read through the segment carefully, noting all strong words and phrases. Record these on analytical Chart R.
2. What is the main subject of Paul in each of the first three paragraphs? Record them on Chart R.
3. Compare "this sect" (v. 22) with "this people" (v. 26).
4. Paul "expounded and testified the kingdom of God, persuading them concerning Jesus" (28:23). Write a list of some of the main doctrines that Paul probably emphasized in his exposition of this theme.

104

ACTS 28:17-31   **Chart R**

17
23
25
30 31

5. How is the last paragraph an appropriate conclusion to the book of Acts? Before answering the question, review Chart C.

• *Applications*
1. example to follow:

_____

2. sin to avoid:

_____

105

3. command to obey:

4. promise to claim:

• *A Topical Study* INSPIRATION OF THE BIBLE

> Well spake the Holy Ghost by Esaias [Isaiah] the prophet
> unto our fathers (18:25).

The *inspiration* of the original text of the books of the Bible
has been defined as

> the work of the Holy Spirit by which, through the instrumental-
> ity of the personality and literary talents of its human authors,
> He constituted the words of the Bible in all of its several parts as
> His written word to men and therefore of divine authority and
> without error in the autographs.[1]

Theories of biblical inspiration concern any of the following:
source, method, time, and end product. The Bible's own testimony to its inspiration speaks only of the first and last of those four.
The exact method and time of inspiration are not developed in
the Scriptures.

The main things taught by the Bible concerning its inspiration are summarized as follows:

I. THE WRITERS WERE INSPIRED ("carried along")

"Holy men from God spoke as they were carried along by the
Holy Spirit" (2 Pet. 1:21, Berkeley). Read also Mark 12:36. The
method of inspiration was not dictation but a mutual interworking
of the divine Spirit and the human mind. The details of the method are not described, just as the details of other miraculous works
of God are not described (indeed, *cannot* be described).

II. THE WRITINGS WERE INSPIRED ("God-breathed")

"Every Scripture is God-breathed" (2 Tim. 3:16, *Amplified*).
This verse teaches that the Bible is a divine product.

1. Kenneth S. Kantzer, "Inspiration," in Merrill C. Tenney, ed., *The Zondervan
Pictorial Bible Dictionary* (Grand Rapids: Zondervan, 1963), p. 380.

III. EXTENT OF INSPIRATION

All Scriptures were inspired (2 Tim. 3:16). This is the plenary view, which applies inspiration to all parts of the Bible, non-religious subjects (e.g., history, science) as well as religious subjects. Inspiration applied to the very words of the originals (verbal inspiration). The net result was inerrancy and infallibility of all the very words of the autographs. (Read Matt. 5:17-19; Luke 16:17; 24:25; John 10:34-35).

IV. ABSOLUTE AUTHORITY OF THE BIBLE

The Bible's main emphasis in its witness concerning itself is its *absolute authority*. A key phrase appearing throughout the Old Testament is "Thus saith the Lord." Read the following passages: Psalms 19:7-14; 119:89, 97, 113, 160; Zechariah 7:12; Matthew 5:17-19; Luke 4:4, 8, 10; 16:17; John 10:34-35; 1 Thessalonians 2:13; Romans 9:15; Galatians 3:8.

V. SOME OTHER WITNESSES OF DIVINE INSPIRATION

1. Christ's use of the Old Testament
2. Fulfilled prophecies
3. Unity of the book
4. Inexhaustible depths
5. Influence of the book
6. Witness of the indwelling Holy Spirit. The Holy Spirit within the believer makes very clear whose voice is speaking through the words of this blessed Book.

Concluding Exercise

For a concluding exercise in Acts, you will find it to be a very interesting study to compare the beginning and end of the book, with reference to Jesus. Record your observations below.

Acts 1:1-11

_____

_____

_____

_____

_____

_____

_____

_____

Paul recedes from view, and Jesus continues to shine, as the narrative of Acts closes. And rightly so. Lange writes of this:

> It is true that, as far as the facts are concerned, we painfully feel the want of all positive and direct information with regard to the manner in which the case of Paul was ultimately decided. However . . . he was merely the herald, and not the Lord and King Himself. Jesus Christ reigns as the King—such is the conclusion of this book.[2]

2. John Peter Lange, *Commentary on the Holy Scriptures, Acts* (Grand Rapids: Zondervan, n.d.), p. 478.

Index of Topical Studies

Bibliography

COMMENTARIES AND TOPICAL STUDIES

Blaiklock, E.M. *The Acts of the Apostles*. Grand Rapids: Eerdmans, 1959.

Bruce, F.F. *The Acts of the Apostles*. Grand Rapids: Eerdmans, 1965.

Harrison, Everett. *Acts: The Expanding Church*. Chicago: Moody, 1976.

Morgan, G. Campbell. *The Acts of the Apostles*. Westwood, N.J.: Revell, 1924.

Pfeiffer, Charles F., and Harrison, Everett F., eds. *The Wycliffe Bible Commentary*. Chicago: Moody, 1962.

Rackham, Richard B. *The Acts of the Apostles*. 13th ed. London: Methuen, 1947.

Ryrie, Charles C. *The Acts of the Apostles*. Chicago: Moody, 1961.

Scroggie, W. Graham. *The Acts of the Apostles*. New York: Harper, n.d.

Walker, Thomas. *The Acts of the Apostles*. Chicago: Moody, 1965.

RESOURCES FOR FURTHER STUDY

Bruce F.F. *The Letters of Paul: An Expanded Paraphrase*. Grand Rapids: Eerdmans, 1965.

Everyday Bible. New Testament Study Edition. Minneapolis: World Wide, 1988.

Jensen, Irving L. *Acts*. Do-it-yourself Bible Studies. San Bernardino: Here's Life, 1984.

————. *Jensen's Survey of the New Testament*. Chicago: Moody, 1981.

New International Version Study Bible. Grand Rapids: Zondervan, 1985.

Ryrie Study Bible. Chicago: Moody, 1985.

Stalker, James. *The Life of St. Paul*. Revised edition. Westwood, N.J.: Revell, 1912.

Strong, James. *The Exhaustive Concordance of the Bible*. New York: Abingdon, 1890.

Thomas W.H. Griffith. *Outline Studies in Acts*. Grand Rapids: Eerdmans, 1956.

Moody Press, a ministry of the Moody Bible Institute,
is designed for education, evangelization, and edification.
If we may assist you in knowing more about Christ
and the Christian life, please write us without obligation:
Moody Press, c/o MLM, Chicago, Illinois 60610.